MW01046706

Essential
Israel

Including the Palestinian Autonomous Territories

by Simon Griver

Above: *the Muslim quarter, Old Jerusalem*

AAA Publishing
1000 AAA Drive, Heathrow, Florida 32746

Above: *Hasidic Jew with child in Me'a She'arim, Jerusalem*

Front cover: *Golan Heights; Bedouin artefact, American Colony Hotel; Dome of the Rock*
Back cover: *Jerusalem artichokes*

Published by AAA Publishing in conjunction with The Automobile Association of Great Britain.

Written by Simon Griver

Library of Congress Catalog Card Number: on file
ISBN 1–56251–497–0

Color separation: Pace Colour, Southampton

Printed and bound in Italy by Printer Trento srl

Contents

About this Book

KEY TO SYMBOLS

- map reference to the maps in the What to See section
- address or location
- telephone number
- opening times
- restaurant or café on premises or near by
- nearest underground train station
- nearest bus/tram route
- nearest overground train station
- ferry crossings and boat excursions
- travel by air
- tourist information
- facilities for visitors with disabilities
- admission charge
- other places of interest near by
- other practical information
- indicates the page where you will find a fuller description

Essential *Israel* is divided into five sections to cover the most important aspects of your visit to Israel.

Viewing Israel pages 5–14
An introduction to Israel by the author.
Israel's Features
Essence of Israel
The Shaping of Israel
Peace and Quiet
Israel's Famous

Top Ten pages 15–26
The author's choice of the Top Ten places to see in Israel, in alphabetical order, each with practical information.

What to See pages 27–90
The five main areas of Israel, each with its own brief introduction and an alphabetical listing of the main attractions.
Practical information
Snippets of 'Did you know…' information
4 suggested walks
3 suggested tours
2 features

Where To... pages 91–116
Detailed listings of the best places to eat, stay, shop, take the children and be entertained.

Practical Matters pages 117–24
A highly visual section containing essential travel information.

Maps
All map references are to the individual maps found in the What to See section of this guide.
For example, Bethlehem has the reference 28B4 – indicating the page on which the map is located and the grid square in which the town is to be found. A list of the maps that have been used in this travel guide can be found in the index.

Prices
Where appropriate, an indication of the cost of an establishment is given by **£** signs:
£££ denotes higher prices, **££** denotes average prices, while **£** denotes lower charges.

Star Ratings
Most of the places described in this book have been given a separate rating:

✪✪✪	Do not miss
✪✪	Highly recommended
✪	Worth seeing

Viewing
Israel

Above: *fresh bagels for sale on a Jerusalem street stall*
Right: *Hasidic Jew in traditional costume*

Simon Griver's Israel

Essential Israel

Holy Sites: Jerusalem's Old City – Western Wall; Via Dolorosa and Holy Sepulchre; Dome of the Rock and El Aqsa Mosque on Temple Mount; Bethlehem's Church of the Nativity and Nazareth's Basilica of the Annunciation

Four Seas: Sunbathe on a Mediterranean beach; float in the Dead Sea; relax by the tranquil Sea of Galilee; explore the exotic marine life of the Red Sea

Landscapes: Jerusalem views, Galilean hills, vast Negev desert expanses

Museums: Israel Museum and Yad Vashem in Jerusalem, Museum of the Jewish Diaspora in Tel Aviv

The Church of the Holy Sepulchre is at the heart of Jerusalem's Christian quarter

Israel is an exhilarating land of contradictions and contrasts that never ceases to surprise.

It is of course the Holy Land to which Moses led the Children of Israel, where Christ preached his sermons and from where Mohammed ascended to heaven. Yet above and beyond the sacred sites Israel is a pulsatingly modern country. Even Jerusalem, with its large ultra-orthodox population, has a vibrant nightlife and high-tech life style. Israelis have built a cohesive and democratic society despite emigrating from Jewish communities in dozens of diverse and mainly authoritarian cultures. The secular Jewish majority often seems profane and decadent rather than pious, and yet a family-orientated society prevails.

Even the Israel-Arab conflict is not as intractable as it sometimes seems. The peace process, despite the political posturing, grinds on because the vast majority of Arabs and Jews prefer compromise to bloodshed.

The country's landscape and climate reflect the diversity of its people, from the west of Jerusalem with its cooler mountain air and forests leading down to the golden beaches of the Mediterranean, to the stark, billowing rocks of the Judean desert, which drop down to the searingly hot and dry Great Syria-Africa Rift Valley. The rolling green hills of the Galilee in the north contrast with the barren and dramatic desert landscapes of the Negev in the south.

At the crossroads between Africa, Europe and Asia the people, the flora and fauna, the climate and the countryside of Israel are a fascinating and unfathomable mixture of all three continents.

Israel's Features

Geography
- Latitude 29–33 degrees north – the same as northern Florida and southern Japan – longitude 35 degrees east
- Area of Israel including the territories under Palestinian control: 21,000sq km
- Highest mountain: Mount Hermon, 2,224m rising to 2,766m in Syrian territory
- Altitude of Jerusalem: 830m
- The Dead Sea is the world's lowest point at 400m below sea level
- The River Jordan is 264km long

Climate
- Average January temperature: 11°C (Jerusalem), 18°C (Tel Aviv), 21°C (Eilat)
- Average July temperature: 29°C (Jerusalem), 30°C (Tel Aviv), 40°C (Eilat)
- Average annual rainfall: 600mm (concentrated between November and March)

People
- Population of Israel in May 2001: 6.4 million
- Largest city: Jerusalem – 680,000 people
- Largest metropolitan area: Tel Aviv-Jaffa and suburbs – 2.3 million residents

Economy
- Israel's annual export trade tops $42 billion; this includes $6 billion in polished diamonds, and a further $25 billion in industrial goods, some 70 per cent of which have high-tech components
- More than 2.5 million tourists visit Israel each year, spending $4.5 billion between them

And
- Israel has the highest per capita number of physicians in the world, with one doctor for every 240 citizens
- With a staggering 40,000 licensed divers, Israel has the highest per capita number of underwater sport participants in the world

A Cultural Mosaic
Israel is home to over 5 million Jews, who have immigrated from every continent. Since 1990 over 900,000 Jews have reached Israel from the former USSR. Israel's Arab minority of more than a million is mainly Muslim but includes 150,000 Christians and 110,000 Druze. There are also more than 2.5 million Palestinians living in the West Bank and Gaza.

Top: *West Bank Palestinian*
Above: *the beach at Ramada*

7

Essence of Israel

You don't have to be religious to appreciate Israel's holy sites. The country has an awesome historical and archaeological heritage from the biblical era as well as a rich store of remains from the neolithic, Roman and Crusader periods. Furthermore, even the most determined sceptic will be moved by the ethereal hillside charms of Jerusalem, the relaxing effect of meditating in the tranquil calm of the Galilee hills or the splendid solitude of the Judean desert. The Mediterranean coast and the Red Sea resort of Eilat invite the more hedonistic, while the Israeli people themselves – informal, impolite and to the point – always enjoy exchanging candid conversation with visitors.

Below: *Socialising around the backgammon board in Tel Aviv*
Bottom: *a goatherd with his flock in the Golan Heights*

THE **10** ESSENTIALS

If you only have a short time to visit Israel, or would like to get a really complete picture of the region, here are the essentials:

• **Visit the Holy Sites** in Jerusalem, Bethlehem, Nazareth and the Galilee. Israel is the cradle of monotheism.

• **See the Dead Sea Scrolls**, the oldest existing version of the Old Testament. Selections from these parchments are exhibited at the Israel Museum.

• **Visit the Yad Vashem Holocaust Museum** to understand the traumatic genocide experienced by European Jewry.

• **Paddle a kayak or float in an inner-tube down the River Jordan**, a fun way to see the countryside (and get accidentally baptised) in what is only a broad stream.

• **Float in the Dead Sea**. Yes, you really float, owing to the water's excessive salt concentration, but any cuts sting like crazy.

• **Ride on a camel** but hold on tight. Tourist camels are always on duty on the Mount of Olives (outside the Seven Arches Hotel), overlooking Jerusalem's Old City.

• **Visit a kibbutz**, though these collectives are having their socialist ethos corrupted by affluence. There are 130,000 people living on 270 kibbutzim in Israel.

• **Bargain in the Arab bazaar** and enjoy the colour and smells of the *souk* in Jerusalem's Old City. Other markets, like Mahane Yehuda in Jerusalem and Carmel Market in Tel Aviv, are a delight for fresh foodstuffs.

• **Eat falafel in pitta.** For a couple of dollars you can stuff your pitta bread full of salad, chips and falafel (fried chick pea balls).

• **See the Red Sea marine life**, including colourful fish of all shapes and sizes and amazing coral formations.

Below: *fresh ingredients on a falafel stall*
Bottom: *the bright colours of the* souk *in Jerusalem's Old City*

The Shaping of Israel

In the 11th century Christian crusaders conquered the Holy Land

c10000 BC
Neolithic man settles the Jordan Valley and Mediterranean coast.

c3000 BC
Canaanite city kingdoms develop, based on trade between Egypt and Mesopotamia.

c2000 BC
Abraham settles in Canaan.

c1300 BC
Moses leads the Israelites out of Egypt.

c1000 BC
King David establishes Jerusalem as his new capital.

c950 BC
King Solomon constructs the Temple. After his death the kingdom divides to form Israel and Judah.

333 BC
Alexander the Great conquers Jerusalem but allows the Jews freedom of worship.

63 BC
The Romans conquer Jerusalem.

37 BC
King Herod assumes the throne as a puppet Roman king.

c5 BC
The birth of Christ.

cAD 30
The crucifixion of Christ.

AD 70
Jewish uprising cruelly quelled by the Romans, who destroy the Temple.

132
Jewish leaders exiled after failed revolt. Jerusalem renamed Aeolina Capitolina.

326
Empress Helena identifies the Holy Sites in Palestine after her son, the Roman emperor Constantine, converts to Christianity.

638
Muslim conquest of Palestine.

691
The Dome of the Rock is built on Temple Mount, followed by the El Aqsa mosque 15 years later.

1009
Caliph Al-Hakim destroys the original Church of the Holy Sepulchre.

1099
Crusaders establish the Kingdom of Jerusalem.

1187
Saladin, Sultan of Egypt and Syria, defeats the Crusaders.

1260
Mamelukes, Asian slave warriors who had taken power in Egypt, capture most of Palestine and centuries of decline begin.

1516
Ottoman Turks capture the Holy Land.

Suleiman the Magnificent

1541
Suleiman the Magnificent completes the Old City walls.

1799
Napoleon occupies parts of the Holy Land.

1878
The first Zionist settlements established in Rishon le-Ziyyon, Petah Tikvah and Rosh-Pinna.

1881
Growing anti-Semitism in Russia forces millions of Jews to emigrate.

1897
Theodore Herzl convenes the first Zionist congress.

1917
The British capture Palestine and declare support for a Jewish homeland.

1920
Arab riots result in British policy U-turn.

1931
Large-scale Jewish immigration from Europe is stopped by the British.

1945
As the Nazi concentration camps are liberated Jewish survivors flock to Palestine, but are interned by the British in Cyprus.

1947
UN votes for the partition of Palestine between a Jewish and an Arab state.

1948
Israel declares its independence.

1949
The War of Independence ends. Egypt annexes Gaza and Jordan seizes East Jerusalem and the West Bank.

1956
Israel captures and returns Sinai following the Suez campaign.

1967
Israel captures East Jerusalem, West Bank, Gaza, Sinai and the Golan Heights in just six days.

1973
Egypt and Syria launch another attack on Israel in the Yom Kippur War.

1977
Menachem Begin

becomes Prime Minister for the Likud, ending 29 years of Labour rule.

1979
Israel signs a peace treaty with Egypt.

1982
Israel invades Lebanon, and the PLO (Palestinian Liberation Organisation) is expelled to Tunis.

1987
Intifada begins.

1991
Iraq launches SCUD missile attacks on Israel during the Gulf War.

1992
Yitzhak Rabin elected Prime Minister.

1993
Yitzhak Rabin signs peace agreement with PLO leader Yasser Arafat.

1994
Israel and Jordan sign a peace agreement.

1995
Yitzhak Rabin assassinated by a Jewish extremist. Shimon Peres becomes Prime Minister.

2000
The peace process falters after Ehud Barak's failure to reach a final status agreement with the Palestinians.

2001
Ariel Sharon elected Prime Minister.

Peace & Quiet

Continental Crossroads

Israel is a nature lover's wonderland because of its unique location between the world's two largest continental landmasses, Eurasia and Africa, so possesses the animal and plant life of each. Moreover, Israel's latitude at the edge of a rain belt means that the flora and fauna reflect different regions, from the Galilee forests (800mm annual rainfall) in the north, to the Negev desert (20mm annually) in the south. Israel's geography has created three quite distinct natural environments – the Mediterranean coast, the inland hills and the Syria-Africa Rift Valley.

This Rift Valley is a strip of land strategically sited between Africa and Eurasia, making it a natural crossing point for millions of migrating birds each spring and autumn. From the Birdwatching Centre in Eilat (► 81) it is possible to view 400 species of migrating bird, including 30 different raptors. Ornithologists can also enjoy Israel's rich indigenous bird life and, at the fish ponds of Ma'agan Michael by the Mediterranean, it is possible to see flamingoes, herons, egrets and gulls.

Bright spring flowers carpet the olive groves of the Golan Heights

Biblical Landscapes

The hillsides around Jerusalem and the Galilee not only offer stunning panoramas, but also a wealth of biblical scenes. The terraced hills contain silver-green olive trees with awesome and ancient gnarled barks, and in the late winter the hillsides are ablaze with almond trees heralding the coming of spring. After the winter rain, spring flowers – red anemones, yellow mustard, pink cyclamen, blue orchids and brown and purple irises – bring the countryside alive with colour. Attentive hikers may glimpse graceful gazelles or a passing tortoise. During this season the orange groves of the coast exude a delicate fragrance.

For those who miss the spring, the peaks of majestic Mount Hermon (► 62) only come into bloom in the summer after the last snow has melted.

Beneath Mount Hermon is the Hula Nature Reserve (➤ 59), where 80 hectares of swamp are inhabited by water buffalo and birds nesting in the papyrus thickets. The original mosquito-infested swamp was drained to make way for farmland, but is now being reflooded because of excessive peat in the soil.

Ibex crossing the rocky crags of 'En Gedi

Desert Vistas

Visitors from the cooler climes of Europe and North America will find the desert more exotic. Israel's deserts are dramatic sweeps of rock with steep canyons carving through them; however, the landscape is far from devoid of life, and tropical oases such as Nahal David near 'En Gedi (➤ 83) are a delight. Look out for the ibex, a mountain goat, and the rabbit-like hyrax scuttling among the rocks. The Makhtesh Ramon (Ramon Crater, ➤ 87), though off the beaten track, is worth seeing to marvel at the layers of colourful rocks that reveal the geological evolution of the planet.

At the Hay Bar Nature Reserve near Eilat (➤ 85) extinct indigenous species, such as the white oryx, have been reintroduced, and a similar process is underway at the Mount Carmel reserve, where deer have been imported.

In sharp contrast to the barren desert, the waters of the Red Sea teem with an incredible range of marine species. Snorkelling and trips in glass-bottomed boats are both available, but for the best introduction visit the Coral World Underwater Observatory (➤ 18).

Somalian wild asses have been reintroduced to the Negev at the Hay Bar Nature Reserve

Israel's Famous

Abraham
The father of the Jewish and Arab peoples, Abraham is seen as the founder of monotheism, the doctrine that there is only one God. Born to a wealthy Mesopotamian family, the book of Genesis tells us that he travelled westwards to settle the Holy Land on God's instructions, after rejecting his father's idolatory. He lived near Beersheba and is buried in Hebron.

The fledgling state's first Prime Minister, David Ben-Gurion

King David

Born just over 3,000 years ago, King David was remarkable as a soldier, poet and prolific womaniser, as the man who wrote the biblical Psalms and extended the borders of Israel from the Red Sea to Syria. He is usually best known, however, for his legendary childhood slingshot victory over Goliath. Rather more significantly, perhaps, in his later years he conquered a Jebusite hilltop enclave, renamed it Jerusalem and moved his capital city there from Hebron. He died in 962 BC.

Jesus Christ

Of the many contemporary accounts only the historian Josephus speaks vaguely of a Galilean preacher, suggesting that Jesus Christ had only a modest impact during his lifetime; however, his determined disciples most effectively disseminated his teachings after his death. Christ was born in Bethlehem in around 5 BC, lived in Nazareth and elsewhere in the Galilee and was crucified in Jerusalem in about AD 30. The sites associated with his life were identified by Helena, the mother of the Emperor Constantine, in the 4th century.

David Ben-Gurion

Born in Russia in 1886, Ben-Gurion emigrated to Palestine in 1906 and was the architect of modern Israel. The founder of the Histadrut trade union movement, the Haganah (forerunner of the Israeli army) and the Jewish Agency (pre-state government) he declared Israeli independence in 1948. Always the radical, Ben-Gurion went to live in a small shack on a Negev kibbutz after resigning as Prime Minister in 1963.

Yitzhak Rabin

Rabin's greatest moment was perhaps the famous handshake with Yasser Arafat on the White House lawn in September 1993, marking the conclusion of the deace deal that won him the Nobel Peace Prize. Born in Jerusalem in 1922, Rabin rose to army chief in 1967 and won a famous victory in the Six Day War. He became Prime Minister in 1974, but resigned in 1977 when his wife admitted having a small but illegal bank account. He was re-elected in 1992, but was assassinated by a Jewish extremist in 1995.

Yitzhak Rabin paid the ultimate price for his attempts to bring peace to the region

Top Ten

Above: *street sign in Old Jaffa*
Right: *Greek Orthodox priest*

1
'Akko (Acre)

✚ 28B6

🕐 Crusader City and
Municipal Museum:
Sun–Thu 8:30–4:45
(opens 7AM May–Oct),
Fri 8:30–12, Sat and
festivals 9–4:45;
Museum of Heroism:
Sun–Thu 8:30–4, Fri
8:30–1. Closed Sat and
festivals

🚌 271, 272 (from Haifa)

🚆 Hourly trains from Haifa

ℹ️ Al-Jazzar Street
☎ (04) 9819 926

Having evolved from Canaanite settlement to Roman campaign base to Crusader stronghold, 'Akko is steeped in history.

'Akko emerged as an important Canaanite port in 1500 BC and later rose to prominence as a Phoenician trading centre. Egyptian ruler Ptolemais II captured the city in 261 BC and renamed it Ptolemais, the name that remained under Roman rule. 'Akko enjoyed a renaissance as a Crusader stronghold (called St Jean d'Acre) from 1104, and in 1291 was the last Crusader fortress in the Holy Land to fall to the Mamelukes, an army of bloodthirsty Asiatic slave warriors. The city remained a regional capital but fell into decline after nearby Haifa was developed as a deep-water port in the 1920s.

Modern 'Akko is a nondescript entity and visitors should focus on the old town, with its fortress wall, moat and sea wall in the southwestern corner of the city. Alexander the Great and Julius Caesar both dwelled here but Napoleon was unable to conquer the city. The Arab market is much smaller, less kitsch and more intimate than Jerusalem's Old City, and the fishing port is delightful.

Most interesting is the subterranean Crusader City, a network of underground halls that was the headquarters of the Knights Hospitallers. The nearby Al-Jazzar Mosque is the most important Israeli mosque after Jerusalem's El Aqsa, while the Municipal Museum, formerly a Turkish bath, documents the city's history.

'Akko has flourished as a port since ancient times

2
Bethlehem

This picturesque hilltop town, overlooking the Judean desert, is an object of pilgrimage for Christians from all over the world.

The entrance to the Grotto of the Nativity – one of the holiest places in the Christian world

Populated since before biblical times, Bethlehem was the burial site of Rachel, Jacob's second wife and the mother of the Children of Israel. Jacob was the son of Isaac, younger son of the prophet Abraham. King David was born here too, but it is as the birthplace of Christ for which the city is best known.

Though Bethlehem is only a 15-minute drive south of Jerusalem, it is necessary to cross the border checkpoint into Palestinian autonomous territory near Rachel's tomb. This is a formality, and generally Bethlehem has been a safe town, but during periods of tension the Israeli army has been known to seal it off.

Bethlehem's 50,000-strong population is divided about fifty-fifty between Muslims and Christians.

Manger Square, in the heart of the city, is the focus for Christian pilgrims. The adjacent **Church of the Nativity** was built in the 6th century by the Emperor Justinian (and later embellished by the Crusaders) on the site of a 4th-century Basilica constructed by Constantine. The outside of the church resembles a fortress more than anything, and the entrance was made very small (for defensive purposes). The Church's crypt – a small, marble-lined cave known as the Grotto of the Nativity – is believed to be the stable where Christ was born. Control of the building is shared, rather acrimoniously, by the Catholic and Greek Orthodox Churches.

Other sites in Bethlehem include the nearby Milk Grotto Church, where, legend has it, the floor is white because Mary's milk splashed to the floor while she was feeding the infant Christ. The field in the village of Bet Sahur on the eastern edge of Bethlehem is believed to be where God announced the birth of Christ to the shepherds.

✝ 28B4

🍴 Wide range of cafés and restaurants (£–£££)

ℹ Manger Square
☎ (02) 277 060 304

❓ On Christmas Eve there is no access to Bethlehem from Jerusalem by car. Special buses shuttle visitors instead

Church of the Nativity

🕐 Daily 7–5; open until after midnight Christmas Eve

♿ No access to crypt

✋ Free

17

3
Coral World, Eilat

Exotic fish in the reef tank aquarium in the underwater observatory

This marine life centre offers visitors a fish's-eye view of the incredible diversity of life to be found in the waters of the Red Sea.

✚ 82B1

✉ Coral Beach, Eilat

☎ (08) 636 4200

🕐 Sat–Thu 8:30–4:30 (5PM Apr–Oct), Fri and eve of festivals 8:30–3. Closed Yom Kippur

🍴 Café and restaurant within complex (££)

🚌 15 from Eilat

ℹ Corner of Yotam and Ha'aravah Streets
☎ (08) 637 2111

♿ Very good

✋ Expensive (submarine extra, very expensive)

The centrepiece of the centre is the underwater observatory, reached by descending a staircase at the pier's end. This circular room has windows below the surface facing out to view the fascinating interaction between the fish and the exquisite coral reef. Fish come in all shapes and sizes, from the tiny yellow box fish to the brilliantly camouflaged, lethal rock fish. Many of the fish are so psychedelic in colour and pattern that it is hard to believe that they are actually real. Absorbing as the observatory is, it is luck that dictates what the visitor actually sees.

An aesthetically constructed aquarium near the entrance to Coral World offers further selected highlights of Red Sea life, while a museum exhibits the fish and coral in comprehensive A to Z fashion accompanied by brief explanations. There is also a pool containing relatively unimpressive sharks and more remarkable rays.

A yellow submarine, moored by the observatory, takes passengers on an hour-long journey beneath the waves, while back on land the Oceanarium screens a 17-minute 'virtual reality' movie in which even the seats move.

4
The Dead Sea
(Yam Ha-Melah)

Located at the lowest point on Earth and surrounded by desert, this unique sea contains so much salt that bathers float.

This part of the Syria-Africa Rift Valley is 400m below sea-level and is surrounded by barren, rocky mountains that yield spectacular views over the salt-laden lake that is the Dead Sea.

The most popular beach is at 'En Gedi, roughly midway along the western shore (the eastern shore is actually in Jordan). The closest bathing point to Jerusalem is at the Qalya water park in the north or the En Fash'ha nature reserve. The hotels at En Boqeq have their own private beaches. Technically it is possible to take a dip anywhere, but the slimy, salty nature of the water makes it desirable to bathe where there are showers provided in order to rinse off immediately after you come out. The water tastes foul and any cuts will sting.

The Dead Sea has a 30 per cent salt content and other minerals beneficial to health such as bromine, iodine and magnesium, which act as sedatives to soothe the nerves and ease psoriasis, rheumatism, arthritis and respiratory complaints. There are also sulphur baths at 'En Gedi and En Boqeq, where various treatments are available, administered by qualified medical personnel. Temperatures rise above 40°C in the summer but the risk of sunburn is reduced because evaporating gases from the sea filter out many of the sun's harmful rays. However, it is best to visit in winter, when average temperatures are around 21°C.

Nearly 77km long and a maximum of 16km wide, the sea has now split into two, owing to evaporation and excessive mining of potassium and bromides; the latter activity earns Israel some $600 million annually in exports.

28C4

Café and restaurant facilities nearby

444 (from Jerusalem and Eilat); 421 (from Tel Aviv via Jerusalem)

'Arad ☎ (08) 995 8144

Good access to sea

Free at 'En Gedi, cheap at En Fash'ha, moderate at Qalya

The salt in the water provides all the support you need to read in the Dead Sea

5
Israel Museum, Jerusalem

Israel's national museum is the leading showcase for the country's archaeology, art and Jewish ethnography, and also houses the Dead Sea Scrolls.

🕇 34A2

✉ Ruppin Boulevard, Jerusalem

☎ (02) 670 8811

🕐 Mon, Wed, Sat and festivals 10–4; Tue 4PM–9PM; Thu 10–9; Fri and eve of festivals 10–2. Closed Sun

🍴 Good café (£) and restaurant (££) on museum complex

🚌 9, 17, 24

ℹ 17 Jaffa Street
☎ (02) 625 8844

♿ Excellent

✋ Moderate

Opened in 1965, the Israel Museum comprises a series of white rectangular pavilions straddling the Jerusalem ridge above the Valley of the Cross. The most conspicuous structure in the complex is the white, breast-shaped building called the Shrine of the Book. Within are showcases exhibiting selections from the Dead Sea Scrolls (➤ 89). The scrolls (discovered by Bedouin shepherds in the 1940s) include the oldest existing copy of the Old Testament and also shed light on the culture of the Essenes, the ascetic Jewish contemporaries of Christ. The tattered parchments can be a disappointment; what renders them fascinating is their age and what they have added to both Jewish and Christian knowledge.

Elsewhere in the museum there are important collections of Jewish art, including over 100 paintings and drawings by acclaimed Jewish artist Marc Chagall, and an extensive exhibition of 19th-century French paintings. There is also a treasure trove of archaeological items from throughout the Middle East, including a tiny decorative pomegranate, the only item known to survive from the First Temple. Also on display are unusual 12,000-year-old artefacts such as woven fabrics, agricultural tools, decorated skulls and carved figurines found in a cave in the Judean Desert. From these items anthropologists have concluded that late Stone Age man was far more advanced than previously thought.

The museum also has an unparalleled collection of Judaica, including entire reconstructions of synagogues from Italy and Poland. The Youth Wing is excellent, with absorbing exhibits and hands-on activities for children.

Some of the ample remains from Israel's 650 years as the Roman province of Judea

6
Jaffa (Yafo)

The tiny alleyways and ancient fishing port of Old Jaffa contrast with the brash modernity of Tel Aviv immediately to the north.

Gathering for a chat in one of Jaffa's many quiet back streets

Old Jaffa became part of the Tel Aviv-Yafo municipality in 1951 and, following a period of extensive restoration, now contains a labyrinth of art galleries and up-market stores.

The port was captured by the Egyptians 3,500 years ago, although archaeological relics have been found near by that predate this period by a further 16,500 years. A small **Museum of Antiquities** exhibits archaeological finds near the attractive orange façade of St Peter's Monastery and the Ottoman clock tower.

Jaffa is featured in the Bible as the port from where Jonah set sail on his ill-fated voyage, and Hiram imported the cedars needed to build the Temple. Despite being the port closest to Jerusalem, there are no sites sacred to Jews here; but Christians revere **Simon the Tanner's House** as the place where the disciple Peter is said to have received divine instruction to preach to non-Jews.

Thought to be the world's oldest harbour, Jaffa's sea traffic now consists of only a few fishing smacks and visiting luxury yachts. At night, however, the excellent fish restaurants around the port attract Tel Aviv's jet-set and create a lively atmosphere set against the high-rise hotels and office buildings that form the northern skyline.

67A1

Good restaurants (££)

46 (from Tel Aviv Central Bus Station); 10 (from Ben Yehuda)

Tel Aviv ☎ (03) 639 5660/516 6188

A series of free summer concerts called Jaffa Nights is held in Kedumim Square in August

Museum of Antiquities

✉ Mifraz Shelomo Street, near Kedumim Square

🕐 Sun, Mon, Thu 9–2, Tue, Wed 9–7. Closed Fri, Sat

♿ Few

✋ Cheap

Simon the Tanner's House

✉ Shimon HaBurski Street, south of Kedumim Square

🕐 Daily 8–7

♿ Few

✋ Cheap

7
Jerusalem's Old City

🕇 35E3

🍴 A wide choice of cheap cafés and restaurants

🚌 1 (Dung Gate); 13, 20, 23, 27, 38 (Jaffa Gate)

ℹ️ By Jaffa Gate
☎ (02) 628 0382

♿ Good. Access to the Western Wall and Temple Mount from Dung Gate only

❓ Procession along Via Dolorosa every Friday at 3PM. The Old City is jam-packed at Christmas and Easter, the Jewish festivals of Passover and Tabernacles and on Friday mornings during Ramadan (May/Jun)

Within Jerusalem's Old City Solomon built the Temple, Christ was allegedly resurrected and Mohammed ascended to heaven.

The square kilometre of the Old City is divided into four quarters – Jewish, Muslim, Christian and Armenian – and can be entered by seven gates. An eighth gate by the Temple Mount (➤ 40), known as the Golden Gate, is blocked up and the belief is that the Messiah will enter Jerusalem from here.

The Temple Mount, the site of the destroyed Temple, is a large complex in the south-eastern corner of the Old City, which contains the resplendent Dome of the Rock (➤ 32) and El Aqsa mosque (➤ 33). The Western Wall (➤ 45) of the Temple Mount, the original retaining wall of the Temple, is considered the holiest site in Judaism. The Via Dolorosa (➤ 45) starts near St Stephen's Gate and winds through the Muslim and Christian quarters to the Church of the Holy Sepulchre.

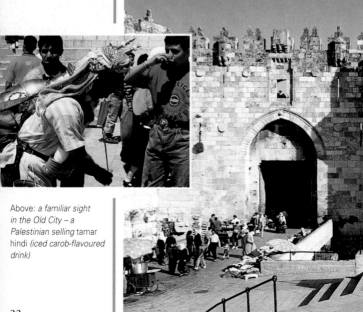

Above: *a familiar sight in the Old City – a Palestinian selling* tamar hindi *(iced carob-flavoured drink)*

The Jaffa Gate and Damascus Gate are the main entrances to the Old City and both lead directly into the Arab *souk* (market). Amid the smell of spices and the exotic, noisy, claustrophobic atmosphere it can be fun to haggle over prices with eager vendors. The New Gate, only made in the 19th century, leads directly into the Christian quarter, while the misnamed Herod's Gate (Herod had nothing to do with it) shows the way to the Muslim quarter. The Zion and Dung Gates offer access to the Jewish quarter, which was rebuilt after being razed by the Jordanians in 1948. The Armenian quarter, in the southwestern corner of the Old City, is a walled city within a walled city and has been inhabited by the Armenian community for over a thousand years.

The Ramparts Walk takes visitors along the walls built by Suleiman the Magnificent in the 16th century.

Below: *looking for bargains in the bustling* Arab *souk*

Left: *the turreted Damascus Gate, constructed in 1537, is the main entrance to the Old City*

8
Nazareth

28B5

Cafés and restaurants
(£–££)

823, 824, 826 (from Tel
Aviv); 331, 441 (from
Haifa)

Casa Nova Street
☎ (04) 657 3003/
0555

Basilica of the Annunciation

Casa Nova Street

☎ (04) 657 0555

🕐 Daily 8:30–11:45, 2–5

❓ Liturgical concerts held
over Christmas period

Nazareth, according to the Bible, is where Jesus spent most of his life; today it is Israel's largest Arab city, with a population of over 70,000.

At the heart of Nazareth is one of the world's holiest Christian shrines, the **Basilica of the Annunciation**; this is built on the site where, according to tradition, Mary and Joseph lived. The basilica is the largest church in the Middle East and was only completed, with no expense spared, in the late 1960s. An 18th-century church was destroyed in order to make way for it, but older remains have been left intact, including parts of a 4th-century baptistry, a 5th-century Byzantine chapel and mosaic floor, and a 12th-century Crusader church.

Visitors overwhelmed by the grandiose style of the basilica may prefer the more humble Church of St Joseph, built in 1914 by the Franciscans on the traditional site of Joseph's carpentry shop, or the nearby Greek Orthodox Church of St Gabriel, which stands, according to Orthodox tradition, above the well where Mary was drawing water when the Archangel Gabriel made the Annunciation.

Above: *at the Greek Orthodox Church of St Gabriel*
Right: *Italian architect Giovanni Muzio designed the modern basilica using different colours of stone*

24

9
Safed (Zefat)

This delightful town, often called the Jerusalem of the Galilee, was once the domain of religious scholars and is now inhabited by artists.

Safed exudes spirituality without being dominated by the religious. Located nearly 1,000m high up in the Galilee mountains, the town has a quaint, airy and mystical charm. Indeed, it was in the Meron Mountains to the west that Jewish scholars in the 2nd and 3rd centuries penned the Jewish mystical texts known as the *Kabbalah*.

Safed itself emerged as a settlement of significance after the Crusaders established a fortress here and its ruins can still be viewed at the highest point in the town. Several centuries later Safed became the world's centre for Jewish scholarship, when a colony of Jewish sages settled here after being expelled from Spain in 1492. The region's first ever printing press was set up here to compile the *Shulhan Aroch*, the compendium of daily Jewish behaviour.

After an earthquake in the 19th century destroyed much of the town, most of the scholars fled to Jerusalem, but the narrow alleyways beneath the town centre retain the medieval synagogues.

In modern times the town has become famous for its artists, who inhabit the quarter adjacent to the medieval synagogues and who draw inspiration from Safed's breath-taking mountain views and the region's mystical and scholarly heritage. Yet in Safed religiosity and the Bohemian, secular nature of the artists seem to gel together harmoniously, and the visitor who strolls through both quarters is not always conscious of the social divide.

Picturesque Safed is often described as 'the city in the sky' in tourist literature

✚ 28B6

🍴 An abundance of restaurants and cafés for all pockets

🚌 963 (from Jerusalem); 891 (from Tel Aviv); 361, 362 (from Haifa)

ℹ️ Municipal Building
☎ (04) 692 7485

♿ Good

❓ The annual Klezmer Festival (Hasidic Music) takes place Jul/Aug

25

10
The Sea of Galilee (Yam Kinneret)

Above and beyond its enchanting beauty, this inland lake and its surrounding settlements are sacred to both Christians and Jews.

The sea is not a sea at all, but rather a lake measuring just 21km by 13km, though still large enough to provide Israel with a third of its water supply. The River Jordan feeds the lake in the north and flows out in the south. Seen at a distance from the surrounding hills, it is possible to make out the harp-shaped outline of the lake (200m below sea level) from which it derives its Hebrew name (*kinor* is Hebrew for harp). Spring is the best time to visit, when the hillsides are greenest and dotted with colourful flowers.

Beautiful though it undoubtedly is, the Sea of Galilee is most remarkable for its religious significance. At Tabigha (► 63), on the northwestern shore, Christ reputedly performed the miracle of the fishes and loaves, while near by, at Capernaum (► 58), he lived for a time and also performed many miracles. Overlooking the lake is the Mount of the Beatitudes (► 62), from where Christ is said to have preached the Sermon on the Mount.

The region also has historical significance for Jews. Tiberias (► 63), the main city on the lake, was where Jewish scholars compiled the *Mishnah* (an important part of the Talmud biblical commentary) in the 2nd and 3rd centuries, and many sages are buried there.

At the point where the River Jordan exits southwards from the lake is Deganya, the first ever kibbutz, established in 1909. Close by is the Yardenit pilgrim site, where many visitors are baptised in the river.

28C5

Try the lakeside fish restaurants in Tiberias (££)

981 (Jerusalem); 830, 835 (Tel Aviv)

Boat tours available on the lake from Tiberias

Habanim Street, Tiberias ☎ (06) 672 5666

Good

Floating across the tranquil waters of Yam Kinneret

What
to See

Top: *Dome of the Rock, Jerusalem*
Right: *camel, Mount of Olives*

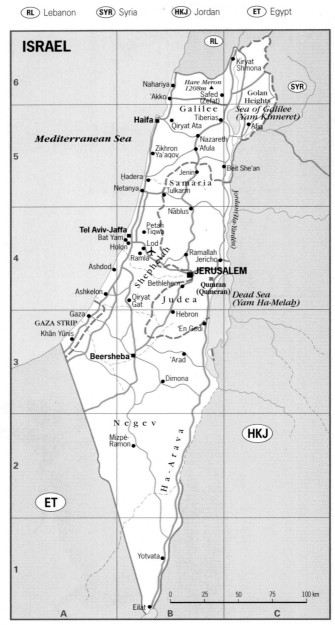

RL Lebanon   SYR Syria   HKJ Jordan   ET Egypt

ISRAEL

Mediterranean Sea

Kiryat Shmona
Nahariya
Hare Meron 1208m ▲
'Akko
Safed (Zefat)
Golan Heights
Galilee
Haifa
Tiberias
Sea of Galilee (Yam Kinneret)
Qiryat Ata
Afiq
Nazareth
Zikhron Ya'aqov
'Afula
Beit She'an
Hadera
Jenin
Samaria
Netanya
Tulkarm
Nablus
Petah Tiqwa
Tel Aviv-Jaffa
Bat Yam
Lod
Holon
Ramallah
Ramla
Jericho
Shephelah
JERUSALEM
Ashdod
Bethlehem
Qumran (Qumeran)
Dead Sea (Yam Ha-Melah)
Ashkelon
Qiryat Gat
Judea
Gaza
Hebron
GAZA STRIP
Khān Yūnis
'En Gedi
Beersheba
'Arad
Dimona
Negev
Mizpé-Ramon
Ha-Arava
Jordan (Ha-Yarden)
HKJ
ET
Yotvata
Eilat

0   25   50   75   100 km

A   B   C

1   2   3   4   5   6

Jerusalem &
Environs

Jerusalem itself is majestically perched on a peak in the Judean Hills over 800m above sea-level. And if Jerusalem is where East meets West, part European and part Asian, then the countryside around the city complements and reinforces this division. Indeed Jerusalem is a continental divide in the strict geographical sense of the term. Water running down west, from the ridge on which central west Jerusalem is built, flows through forests to the Mediterranean and Atlantic; water running east passes down desert canyons and exits into the Red Sea and Indian Ocean.

The countryside is attractive, but more striking are the desert landscapes to the east – a barren, spectacular rock desert that has long been a favourite haunt of hermits and monastics. The Jerusalem Forest to the west of the city reputedly has six million trees, a living memory of the Jews who perished in the Holocaust. Along the mountain summits to the north and south of Jerusalem are the major Palestinian cities – Bethlehem and Hebron to the south and Ramallah and Nablus to the north.

*' By far the most
interesting half-acre on the
face of the earth. '*

W M THOMSON on the Church of
the Holy Sepulchre
The Land and the Book (1859)

———————●———————

Jerusalem

Jerusalem is a harmonious mosaic. Divided both religiously and ethnically, the Holy City nevertheless holds together to form a cohesive entity. Superficially this harmony has been enhanced by the fact that Jerusalem's buildings are faced with stone, allowing a myriad of architectural styles from down the centuries to blend together amid the craggy hillsides, enhancing those romantic mountain views.

This harmony runs deeper than mere externals. The city's 600,000 residents are still deeply divided, even though the walls between the Arab and Jewish parts of the city were knocked down after reunification in 1967. Moreover, the Jewish residents are bitterly split between a large minority of black-clad, ultra-orthodox Jews and the mainstream Jewish population, which includes the secular, traditional and orthodox. Despite the tensions, however, there seems to be a mutual pact not to let the acrimony spill over into bloodshed, and terrorist outrages are almost never committed by Jerusalemites themselves.

For visitors, less concerned with the complexities of contemporary Jerusalem, this is first and foremost the Holy City that is home to the sites so sacred to Jews, Christians and Muslims. In addition, Jerusalem is also the capital of modern Israel and the home of national institutions like the Knesset (Parliament), Israel Museum, Hebrew University and Yad Vashem Holocaust Memorial and Museum. Yet the city is not weighed down by all this religion and intellectual pursuit and the bustling nightlife is something of a revelation, with nightbirds packing out the night spots of the Russian Compound well into the early hours of the morning.

Jerusalem cityscape seen from the Mount of Olives

What to See in Jerusalem

CHURCH OF THE HOLY SEPULCHRE ✪✪✪

The most important shrine in Christendom, this is where the Orthodox and Catholic churches believe Christ was crucified, buried and resurrected. However, many Protestants dispute that this was the site of Calvary and suggest it was located rather at the Garden Tomb (➤ 33). The Church itself is not especially impressive or attractive, but is a confusing place crammed with icons, murals and ritual works of art.

Constructed in 1149 by the Crusaders on the site of a Byzantine chapel, the Church contains the last five Stations of the Cross of the Via Dolorosa (➤ 45), the route Christ was believed to have taken carrying the cross to his crucifiction. According to tradition, the tenth and eleventh Stations (points along the route) at the top of the staircase to the right of the entrance are where Christ was stripped and nailed to the cross. At the adjacent twelfth Station he was crucified and then his body was handed back to Mary at the adjoining thirteenth Station. Down the stairs and back past the entrance is a narrow, low passage leading to the tomb of Christ itself.

✝ 35E3
✉ End of Shuq Ha-Tsabaim (Souk ed-Dabagha), Old City
🕐 Daily, dawn to dusk
♿ Few
🚌 1, 3, 13, 19, 20, 23, 38 (to Jaffa Gate)
🎫 Free

Did you know?

The keys to the Church of the Holy Sepulchre have been held by the same Muslim family for centuries. This is because the six churches who own the building – Roman Catholic, Greek Orthodox, Ethiopian, Armenian, Syrian and Coptic – all distrust each other.

Chapel of the Crucifixion

CITY OF DAVID ✪

Much of the original city built by David is actually just outside the Old City walls, immediately east of the Dung Gate. The city was presumably established here because of the water below in the Gihon Spring; it is possible to cross the road and walk down the steps to Hezekiah's Tunnel and wade along (with a candle) the conduit that brought ancient Jerusalem its water. The recently spruced-up archaeological park is nevertheless unexceptional save for the fact that this was King David's Jerusalem.

✝ 35F2
✉ Ma'ale Ha-Shalom Street
🕐 Sun–Thu 9–5, Fri 9–1. Closed Sat and festivals
♿ None
🚌 1, 2, 38
🎫 Cheap

Right: *the Dome of the Rock's dome was only covered with gold in 1994*
Above: *window detail*

➕ 35F3
✉ Temple Mount, Old City
🕐 Sat–Thu from after dawn prayers to before dusk. Closed during midday prayers, Fri and Muslim festivals
🍴 Near by (£)
🚌 1, 38 (Dung Gate)
♿ Very good
⛔ Moderate

➕ 34C4
🍴 A wide range of restaurants from very cheap to very expensive
🚌 4, 5, 6, 7, 9, 14, 15, 17, 18, 19, 20, 21, 23, 30, 31, 32
♿ Excellent

DOME OF THE ROCK ✪✪✪

This exquisite edifice was built on the Temple Mount in AD 691 by Caliph Abd el-Malik, although the current exterior was only completed in the 16th century by Suleiman the Magnificent. The original shrine was built above the rock from which Muslims believe Mohammed ascended to heaven and on which Abraham intended to sacrifice his son Isaac (in the book of Genesis). The striking exterior, with its tile ornamentation, geometrical and floral themes in delicate shades of blue and green and attractive calligraphy from the Koran, demonstrates how Islam has developed abstract art forms in the need to avoid graven images. Inside, the building is no less resplendent: golden mosaics line the interior of the dome, which soars above the huge black rock that gives the mosque its name.

DOWNTOWN JERUSALEM ✪✪

The area immediately west of the Old City, along Jaffa Road, is sometimes called the New City or Downtown Jerusalem; at its heart is the bustling Ben Yehuda Street Mall, alive with streetside cafés, cheap eateries, souvenir shops, buskers and artists. Nahalat Shiva, at the bottom of Ben Yehuda, is one of the oldest neighbourhoods outside of the Old City, built in 1869 and introducing Spanish-style red roofs to the Holy Land. Salomon and Rivlin Streets are also pedestrianised and contain many popular restaurants. Across Jaffa Street is the Russian Compound, dominated by the distinctive green roofs of the Holy Trinity Cathedral. This is the place to be from midnight onwards, as the adjacent Monbaz and Heleni Hamalakh Streets contain dozens of bars.

EL AQSA MOSQUE

✪✪✪

This silver-domed building on the southern edge of the Temple Mount is the most important mosque in Jerusalem and was built in AD 705 by the Umayyad caliph. The Crusaders later converted it into a palace for the Templars but the Egyptian ruler Saladin transformed the building back to a mosque again after conquering Jerusalem in 1187. In contrast to the nearby Dome of the Rock, El Aqsa is a rather austere building, with a somewhat shabby façade for one of the most important mosques in Islam. The interior is more lavish, especially the dozens of Persian rugs that carpet the floor. A chipped pillar near the entrance was caused by the gunfire that assassinated Jordan's King Abdullah in 1951; his grandson and successor, Hussein, was praying next to him at the time. In 1969 an Australian Christian fanatic succeeded in inflicting major damage to El Aqsa when he set fire to the mosque.

- ✚ 35F3
- ✉ Temple Mount, Old City
- ☎ (02) 6281248
- 🕐 Sun–Thu after dawn prayers until just before dusk. Closed during midday prayers, Fri and Muslim festivals
- 🚌 1, 38
- ♿ Excellent
- 🎟 Moderate

Above: *less ornamented than the Dome of the Rock, El Aqsa serves primarily as a prayer hall*

GARDEN TOMB

✪✪

The Garden Tomb is also known as the Protestant Holy Sepulchre, although the English group who own the site insist that there is no definite evidence that this really was the location of the crucifixion. It was the 19th-century British general Gordon (some say annoyed that the Church of the Holy Sepulchre was owned by the Catholic and Eastern Orthodox churches) who suggested that the presence of a 1st-century tomb and a skull-like shaped hillock could mean that this was Calvary. In any event, the garden's tranquillity in the heart of Jerusalem makes this an oasis of serenity and an ideal place for meditation.

- ✚ 35E4
- ✉ Nablus Road (several hundred metres from the Damascus Gate)
- 🕐 Mon–Sat 8–1, 3:30–5. Closed Sun
- 🍴 Near by (£)
- 🚌 12, 27
- ♿ Good
- 🎟 Free

33

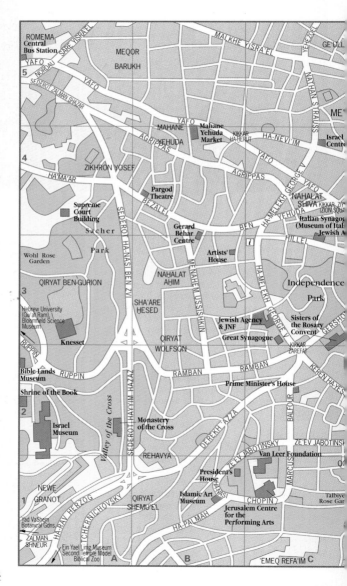

ROMEMA
Central Bus Station
YAFO
NORDAU
SEDEROT ZALMAN SHAZAR
MEQOR BARUKH
SAREY YISRA'EL
YAFO
MALKHE YISRA'EL
GE'ULL
VEHEZEL
NATHAN STRAUSS
GE'ULL

5

YAFO
MAHANE YEHUDA
AGRIPPAS
Mahane Yehuda Market
KIKKAR HAHERUT
HA-NEVI'IM
YAFO
ME'
Israel Centre

4
ZIKHRON YOSEF
HA'MA'AR
AGRIPPAS
YAFO
HA-MELEKH GEORGE V

Pargod Theatre
BEZALEL
NAHALAT SHIVA
KIKKAR ZIY
ITZION SOUA

Supreme Court Building
SEDEROT HANASI BEN ZVI
Sacher
Wohl Rose Garden
Park
Gerard Behar Centre
BEN YEHUDA
HA-MELEKH GEORGE V
Italian Synago
(Museum of Ital
Jewish A

QIRYAT BEN-GURION
NAHALAT AHIM
Artists' House
i
HILLEL

3
Hebrew University (Giv'at Ram), Bloomfield Science Museum
Knesset
SHA'ARE HESED
MENAHEM USSISHKIN
Independence
Park

RUPPIN
QIRYAT WOLFSON
Jewish Agency & JNF
Great Synagogue
HA-MELEKH GEORGE V
Sisters of the Rosary Convent
GERSHO
KIKKAR ZAREFAT
KEREN HAYES

Bible Lands Museum
RUPPIN
RAMBAN
RAMBAN

Shrine of the Book

2
Valley of the Cross
SEDEROT HAYYIM HAZAZ
Monastery of the Cross
Prime Minister's House
BALFOUR

Israel Museum
REHAVYA
DERERH AZZA
ZE'EV JABOTINSKY
Van Leer Foundation
ZE'EV JABOTINS

President's House
MARCUS

NEWE GRANOT
HA-RAV HERZOG
TCHERNICHOVSKY
QIRYAT SHEMU'EL
Islamic Art Museum
HA-NASI
CHOPIN
Jerusalem Centre for the Performing Arts
Talbiye Rose Gar

1
Yad VaShem Botanical Gdns.
ZALMAN SHNEUR
Ein Yael Living Museum, Second Temple Model, Biblical Zoo
HA-PAL'MAH
'EMEQ REFA'IM

A
B
C

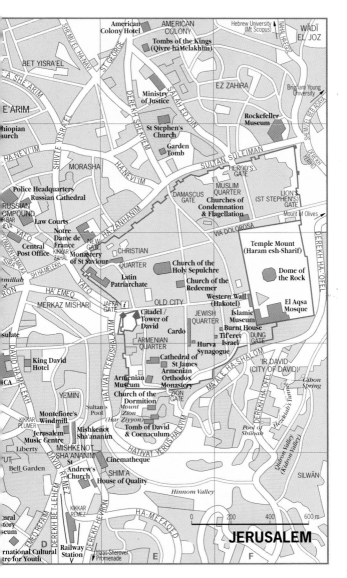

American
Colony Hotel
AMERICAN
COLONY
Hebrew University
(Mt Scopus)
WĀDĪ
EL JOZ
NAHAL HEGO

SHEMU'EL HANAVI
ST GEORGE
DEREKH SHEKHEM
Tombs of the Kings
(Qivre haMelakhim)
SALAH ED-DIN

BET YISRA'EL

Ministry
of Justice

EZ ZAHIRA

Brigham Young
University

SHEMU'EL BEN ADAYA

'A SHE'ARIM

E'ARIM

hiopian
urch

SHIVTE YISRA'EL

MORASHA

HA-NEVI'IM

St Stephen's
Church

Garden
Tomb

Rockefeller
Museum

HA-NEVI'IM

SULTAN SULEIMAN

HEROD'S
GATE

DEREKH YERIHO

Police Headquarters
Russian Cathedral

RUSSIAN
OMPOUND
R-BAR
IEVA

MUSLIM
QUARTER

DAMASCUS
GATE

Churches of
Condemnation
& Flagellation

LION'S
(ST STEPHEN'S)
GATE

Mount of Olives

Law Courts

YAFO

Central
Post Office

SIRA'A

Notre
Dame de
France

NEW
GATE

KIKKAR
ZAHAL

Monastery
of St Saviour

CHRISTIAN

QUARTER

VIA DOLOROSA

Temple Mount
(Haram esh-Sharif)

DEREKH HA-'OFEL

DEREKH HA-TZANHANIM

SH HA-MELEKH

Latin
Patriarchate

Church of the
Holy Sepulchre

Dome of
the Rock

millah
l
RON

HA-'EMEQ

YAFO

Church of the
Redeemer

MERKAZ MISHARI

JAFFA
GATE

OLD CITY

Western Wall
(Hakotel)

Islamic
Museum

El Aqsa
Mosque

sulate

Citadel /
Tower of
David

JEWISH
QUARTER

Cardo

Burnt House
Tiferet
Israel

DUNG
GATE

DAVID HAMELEKH

HATIVAT YERUSHALAYIM

ARMENIAN
QUARTER

Hurva
Synagogue

ICA

King David
Hotel

Cathedral of
St James

'IR DAVID
(CITY OF DAVID)

Gihon
Spring

YEMIN

Armenian
Museum

Armenian
Orthodox
Monastery

MA'ALE HA-SHALOM

ZION
GATE

Church of the
Dormition

Montefiore's
Windmill

KIKKAR
PLUMER

Sultan's
Pool

Mount
Zion
(Har Tziyyon)

Pool of
Shiloah

Hezekiah's Tunnel

SILWĀN

Jerusalem
Music Centre

Mishkenot
Sha'ananim

Tomb of David
& Coenaculum

Qidron Valley
(Kidron Valley)

Liberty

MISHKENOT
SHA'ANANIM

St
Andrew's
Church

Cinematheque

HATIVAT YERUSHALAYIM

'UT

Bell Garden

DEREKH HA-MEFARBEL

SHIM'A
House of Quality

Hinnom Valley

ural
tory
eum

DEREKH HEVRON

KIKKAR
REMEZ

HA-METAQED

0   200   400   600 m

EMEQ REFA'IM

rnational Cultural
tre for Youth

Railway
Station

DEREKH HE-HON

Haas-Sherover
Promenade

JERUSALEM

E   F

35

+ 35D1
- Naomi Street, Abu Tor or
  Daniel Yanovski Street,
  East Talpiot
- Café on the walkway (£)
  and a restaurant on the
  promenade (££)
- 7, 8, 48
- Excellent

Above: *the spectacular
views from Haas-
Sherover Promenade*

+ 34A3
- Corner of Rothschild and
  Kaplan Streets
- (02) 675 3333
- Sun and Thu 8:30–2:30
  (tours). Mon–Wed
  afternoon and evening
  during debates. Entrance
  allowed only on
  presentation of passport
- Self-service cafeteria (£)
  and restaurant (££) on
  site
- 9, 24
- Free

HAAS-SHEROVER PROMENADE ✪✪

This tastefully designed walkway and terraced garden offers a superb view of Jerusalem, a view that stretches to the Jordan Valley in the clearer light of the winter. Completed in the 1980s, the promenade and its sloping hillside gardens reflect contemporary Jerusalem landscaping at its aesthetic best. The walkway stretches several kilometres from Abu Tor to East Talpiot, skirting the St Clair Monastery, and finishes at Government House, formerly the British governor's residence and today the UN's Middle East HQ. This is believed to be the Hill of the Evil Counsel, where the house of Caiphas, the high priest who paid Judas to betray Christ, was located.

KNESSET ✪✪

The Knesset, Israel's parliament, is a 120-seat single chamber assembly elected every four years by proportional representation. The neo-classical building was completed in 1966; the reception hall is adorned by a large tapestry by Jewish artist Marc Chagall, depicting Jewish history. Peculiarly, the plenary chamber is downstairs from the main entrance. This is because the entrance plaza was originally planned to be to the south, rather than the north of the building, and it was only later realized that Jordanian artillery near Bethlehem would be able to shell the entrance. This threat was removed a year later during the Six Day War but the entrance remains on the north side.

Opposite the Knesset is a carved bronze *menorah* (candelabrum), donated by the British parliament. Behind this is the Wohl Rose Garden, which in the spring and autumn is ablaze with 450 different species of roses.

ME'A SHE'ARIM ⭐⭐

The bastion of ultra-orthodox Jewry, this quarter is a world apart, inhabited by black-clad members of various fundamentalist Jewish sects, some of whom are opposed to the very existence of Israel. The narrow streets, alleyways and courtyards, as well as the form of dress, are a transposition from Eastern Europe in the late middle ages. Modest dress is obligatory for women, both residents and visitors, and no photography or traffic is permitted on Friday night or Saturday. Residents can react violently towards visitors who infringe these rules.

🚩 34C5
🕐 Streets closed to traffic on sabbaths and festivals
🍴 Restaurants near by (£)
🚌 1, 3, 4, 9, 15, 25, 27
♿ Good

MOUNT OF OLIVES ⭐⭐⭐

The Mount of Olives is the most sacred site in Jerusalem outside the Old City and from lookout points offers a stirring panorama of the Temple Mount to the west. The Jewish cemetery that dominates the hillside has special significance for orthodox Jews, who believe that when the Messiah comes those buried on the hillside will be the first to return to life. The Mount of Olives is also revered by Christians because at the foot of the hill is the Garden of Gethsemane, in Christian belief the site of Christ's betrayal, in front of the Franciscan Church of All Nations. Also known as the Basilica of the Agony, the church has a large mosaic façade depicting Christ mediating between God and the people. Opposite Gethsemane is the Greek Orthodox Church of Mary's Tomb, where some believe the mother of Christ is buried. On the hillside above is the Russian Orthodox Church of St Mary Magdalene with its five pleasingly proportioned gold onion domes, which was built by Tsar Alexander III in 1873.

🚩 35F4
✉ to the east of Jerusalem
🍴 Near by (£)
🚌 99, 27 (walk down from Rockefeller Museum)
♿ Good
❓ Camel rides are available from the Mount of Olives lookout

The Church of All Nations at the foot of the Mount of Olives is remarkable for its splendid Byzantine-style façade

Around Jerusalem's Hilltops

Drive north along Ma'ale Ha-Shalom, turning left onto Jericho Street and then right to the Hebrew University.

The Hebrew University, perched on top of Mount Scopus (► 39), was opened in 1925. The view

The Hebrew University surveys the city from the top of Mount Scopus

to the south is one of the Old City, while to the east is the panorama of the Judean Desert. Continue to the Mormon University's Brigham Young campus, which blends handsomely into the hills, and join one of the worthwhile hourly tours. On the far side of the village of A-Tur is the Mount of Olives lookout (► 37).

Distance
35km (including Bethelehem)

Time
Allow 6–8 hours including stops; 2 hours without stops

Start/end point
Dung Gate
➕ 35F3

Lunch
Trattoria Italiana, Botanical Garden Restaurant (££)
☎ (02) 679 3795

Drive down the hill of El-Mansuriya and turn right at the Garden of Gethsemane along Jericho Street. Skirt the Old City walls along Sultan Suleiman and Ha-Zanhanim, then continue along Shelomo Ha-Melekh, Agron and Ramban and finally turn left into Hayyim Hazaz to the Monastery of the Cross.

The Monastery of the Cross was built by the Georgian Orthodox Church in 1038 and derives its name from the surrounding olive groves, which purportedly provided the wood for the Cross. Today the monastery is a college for Orthodox priests.

Turn right down Ha-Rav Herzog, then right again down Zalman Schneur to reach the Botanical Gardens.

These are pleasantly situated below the science campus of the Hebrew University. The Italian restaurant by the lake is a pleasant place to lunch.

Drive up Azza, right into Keren Ha-Yesod and via David Remez, Hebron Street and Daniel Yanovski to Haas-Sherover Promenade (► 36). If time permits, travel south along Hebron Street to Bethlehem (► 17).

MOUNT SCOPUS ⭐⭐

The hilltop ridge to the north of the Mount of Olives (▶ 37) is dominated by the Hebrew University, which, along with the nearby Hadassah Hospital, was abandoned between 1948 and 1967 when it was cut off from the rest of Jewish Jerusalem. The University's Law and Archaeology faculties returned after the Six Day War and the Humanities and Social Sciences in 1982. Mount Scopus affords a marvellous view of the Old City and it was from these heights that most opposing armies have conquered the Holy City. The University's amphitheatre commands a spectacular view of the Judean Desert, and also worth visiting is the new campus of the Brigham Young Mormon University. The adjacent neighbourhood of French Hill, named after a brief visit by Napoleon's army, can be found just past the meticulously maintained lines of graves at the British Commonwealth War Cemetery.

🔲 35F5
🕐 Hebrew University: Sun–Fri AM; Mormon University: Mon–Sat
🍴 Nearby cafés and restaurants (£)
🚌 4a, 9, 28
♿ Excellent
✋ Free

Below: *the many churches on Mount Zion are built over largely apocryphal religious sites*

MOUNT ZION ⭐

Since the Babylonian exile, Zion was the name taken by Jews to symbolise their yearning to return to Jerusalem. Hence the 19th-century political movement urging a return to Israel called itself Zionism. This small hillock in the southeastern corner of the Old City actually contains little of Jewish interest other than a chamber that claims to be King David's tomb but is generally believed to be unauthentic. The Coenaculum above it is revered by many Christians as the site of Christ's Last Supper, while the whole area is dominated by the nearby Church of the Dormition, built on the site where Mary is believed to have died.

🔲 35E2
🕐 Coenaculum: Sun–Thu & Sat 8–5 (closes at 6 in summer), Fri 8–2
🍴 None
🚌 1, 38 (Dung Gate); 13, 19, 20, 23
♿ Few
✋ Free

Did you know ?

Suleiman the Magnificent mistakenly left Mount Zion outside the Old City walls when they were built in the 16th century. It is said that he had his chief engineer beheaded for the error.

✠ 34A2

Bible Lands Museum
✉ Granot St
☎ (02) 561 1066
🕐 Sun–Tue, Thu 9:30–5:30,
   Wed 9:30–9:30, Fri
   9:30–2, Sat 11–3
🚌 9, 24, 28

Bloomfield Science Museum
✉ Ruppin Boulevard
☎ (02) 654 4888
🕐 Mon, Wed, Thu 10–6,
   Tue 10–8, Fri 10–1, Sat
   10–3
♿ Excellent
🗿 Moderate

Right: *Byzantine church
chancel screen, Bible
Lands Museum*

✠ 35F3
🕐 Just after dawn prayers
   until just before dusk.
   Closed for midday
   prayers
🚌 1, 38 (Dung Gate)
♿ Good
🗿 Moderate

Below: *model of the
Second Temple,
Holyland Hotel*

MUSEUM MALL ✪✪✪

This boulevard to the west of the city contains the Israel Museum (➤ 20), the **Bible Lands Museum** and the **Bloomfield Science Museum**. A Natural History Museum is under construction.

The Bible Lands Museum promotes a deeper understanding of the Bible by exhibiting objects relating to the various cultures – Sumerian, Assyrian, Babylonian, Israeli, Egyptian, Persian, Greek and Roman – that laid the foundations for Judeo-Christian civilisation. The nearby Bloomfield Science Museum focuses on science and technology and makes the subject hands-on fun for children.

TEMPLE MOUNT ✪✪✪

Known as Har Habayit in Hebrew and Haram esh-Sharif in Arabic, Temple Mount is both the focal point of Jewish and Muslim attachment to Jerusalem and a bitter bone of contention between religious and nationalistic fundamentalists in both camps. Confrontation has been diffused by a rabbinical ruling, refusing Jews entry to the site on the grounds that they might tread on the Holy of Holies, the Temple sanctuary of old, where the High Priest would speak with God.

It was on Temple Mount that Solomon built the first Temple to house the Ark of the Covenant in 953 BC. It is

also believed that the world was created here, from the rock within the Dome of the Rock (► 32), which is also where Abraham attempted to sacrifice Isaac, and from where Mohammed ascended to heaven. The First Temple was destroyed by the Babylonians in the 6th century BC but was subsequently rebuilt on a grand scale (the Second Temple Model, near the Holyland Hotel in West Jerusalem, gives a good impression of the complex's size). Ten gates lead into Temple Mount, including the Moors' Gate by the Western Wall (► 45), the only surviving part of the Temple complex that was left standing by the Romans.

After the Romans destroyed the Temple, the site remained neglected until Caliph Abd el-Malik built the Dome of the Rock in AD 691; his son went on to build El Aqsa mosque (► 33).

Temple Mount remains in the hands of the Wakf Islamic authorities, who charge a single entry fee for the Dome of the Rock, El Aqsa and the Islamic Museum, which tells the story of Muslim life in Jerusalem. Solomon's Stables, a cavernous hall in the southeastern corner, was formerly used as stables by the Crusaders and is now a mosque; entry is barred to non-Muslims.

Below: *the high, slender Tower of David rises above the medieval fortress known as the Citadel*

TOWER OF DAVID MUSEUM OF THE HISTORY OF JERUSALEM ✪✪

The Tower of David was Jerusalem's main fortress and garrison for 3,000 years yet shares only a mythical link with the founder of Jerusalem. Archaeological excavations around the site show the history of Jerusalem from biblical times, while the interior halls contain state-of-the-art exhibits depicting Jerusalem's historical development. There is also a scale model of 19th-century Jerusalem made from zinc, and a sound and light show telling the story of the Holy City. From the Tower itself a wonderful view can be had of the Old City and surrounding hills.

🔲 35E3
✉ Jaffa Gate
☎ (02) 626 5333 (24hr information)
🕐 Sun–Thu 10–4; Sat, holidays and holiday eves 10–2. Closed Fri
🍴 Near by (£)
🚌 13, 20, 23
♿ Good
💰 Expensive

In the Know

If you only have a short time to visit Israel, or want to get a real flavour of the country, here are some ideas:

10
Ways to Be a Local

Use the word *shalom*. It means hello and good-bye as well as peace.

Dress casual: suits and ties and other formal dress are out.

Overtake on the inside and honk your horn frequently. Israelis are not cautious drivers.

Nurse one drink all night as Israelis are not big drinkers and don't like drunkenness.

Eat a pitta stuffed with falafel or *schwarma*, or use it to mop up food.

Don't tip taxi drivers – Israelis don't.

Speak on a cellular phone whilst on the beach, in the supermarket, or on a bus. When driving, Israelis are always on the phone.

Offer something sweet to a stranger's child – Israelis cannot resist indulging a cute child.

Play rackets on the beach, a popular local beach game that is a cross between tennis and table tennis.

Stay out after midnight, when the Israeli nightlife and the action in the clubs and pubs really gets going.

10
Good Places to Have Lunch

Abu Shukri (£)
✉ Ha-Gai Street corner of Via Dolorosa, Old City, Jerusalem ☎ (02) 627 1538. Famous for its houmous.

La Barracuda (£)
✉ Commercial Centre, Eilat ☎ (08) 637 6222. Good seafood.

Eucalyptus (££)
✉ 4 Safra Square, Jerusalem ☎ (02) 624 4331. Traditional food from the region.

Galei Gil (££)
✉ Tiberias waterfront ☎ (04) 672 0699. Try St Peter's fish, a species unique to the Sea of Galilee.

Moshav Amirim (££)
☎ (04) 698 9572. Vegetarian settlement near Safed.

Nof Chinese Restaurant (££)
✉ Nof Hotel, 101 Hanassi Boulevard, Haifa ☎ (04) 835 4311. Enjoy the food and the superb view of the bay.

Philadelphia East (££)
✉ 9 Azzahra Street, Jerusalem ☎ (02) 628 9770. You can dine just on the *mezze*.

Taboon (££)
✉ Old Jaffa Port ☎ (03) 681 6011. Try the oven-baked fish.

Tel Aviv Central Bus Station (£)
✉ Matalon Street, Tel Aviv. Stuff as much as you can into a pitta for a nominal sum.

Zion (££)
✉ 4 Peduim Street, Tel Aviv ☎ (03) 517 8714. The pick of the eateries in the Yemenite quarter.

Zion Square by night

Windsurfing off the coast of Tel Aviv

10
Archaeological Sites

- **Avdat** (Nabatean, Byzantine)
- **Beit She'an** (Byzantine, ➤ 55)
- **Caesarea** (Roman, Crusader, ➤ 55)
- **City of David** (biblical, ➤ 31)
- **Eqron** (Kibbutz Ravid near Ashdod; Philistine)
- **Hazor** (Upper Galilee; (23 civilisations)
- **Jericho** (neolithic, Ummayad, ➤ 48)
- **Masada** (Herodian/ Roman, ➤ 86)
- **Megiddo** (20 civilisations from Canaanite and biblical, ➤ 60)
- **Nimrod Castle** (Golan Heights; Crusader, ➤ 59)

10
Top Activities

Diving: see the Red Sea marine life in the flesh. Contact Red Sea Divers, Caravan Hotel, Eilat ☎ (08) 637 3145/6.

Golf: Israel's only course is at Caesarea ☎ (04) 636 1174.

Hiking: from the Galilee hills to the Negev wadis. Details from SPNI ✉ 13 Helena Hamalka, Jerusalem ☎ (02) 623 2936.

Horse riding in the Judean Hills: Contact King David Ranch ✉ Neve Ilan (near Jerusalem) ☎ (02) 534 0535.

Inner-tubing: float down the River Jordan on an inner tube. Information from Kibbutz Sde Nehemya, Upper Galilee ☎ (04) 694 6010.

Katarafting: a cross between a canoe and a katamaran. Contact Kibbutz Kfar Hanasi, Upper Galilee ☎ (04) 691 4992.

Kayaking: be like an eskimo in the Middle East. Find out more from Kibbutz Kfar Blum, Upper Galilee ☎ (04) 694 8657.

Rock climbing: climb the mountains by the Dead Sea. Contact Kibbutz Mizpé Shalem ☎ (02) 994 5111.

Skiing: Hermon ski site is open Dec–May ☎ (06) 698 1339.

Windsurfing: Contact Octopus ✉ Tel Aviv Marina ☎ (03) 527 1440.

Rock climbing at Mizpé-Ramon

Through the Old City

Distance
2km

Time
3–4 hours, including relatively brief visits to the countless sites en route

Start point
Jaffa Gate
✚ 35E3

End point
Damascus Gate
✚ 35E4

Lunch
Abu Shukri (£)
✉ Ha-Gai Street, corner of Via Dolorosa
☎ (02) 627 1538

Enter the Old City through the Jaffa Gate and go straight ahead into the Arab souk (market). After several hundred metres turn right into Ha'Kardo.

The Cardo, which links the Muslim Quarter with the Jewish Quarter, is the original main north–south street from Byzantine times and has been excavated and restored. The staircase at the end leads up to Beit El Street. The huge arch rising above this peaceful square is a monument to the Hurva, the largest synagogue in the old City, which was destroyed in 1948. Across the plaza on the left is the Burnt House, a restoration of the home of the priestly Kathros family who lived in Roman times.

Opposite the end of Tiferet Yisra'el is a staircase called Ma'alot Rabi Yehuda Halevi, which leads down to the Western Wall (➤ 45).

The carefully restored arch is a striking symbol of Hurva's past glory

In front of the Western Wall is the Hasmonean Tunnel (advance bookings only ☎ (02) 627 1333). This is the original street from Second Temple times; it runs beneath the western perimeter of the Temple Mount and exits on to the Via Dolorosa (➤ 45) by the second Station. (Otherwise go round along Ha-Gai Street and rejoin the Via Dolorosa at the Austrian Hospice). Stroll along the Via Dolorosa, stopping for a lunch of houmous, pitta and salad at Abu Shukri on the corner of Ha-Gai at the fifth Station of the Cross. A fascinating way to enter the Church of the Holy Sepulchre (➤ 31) is via the Ethiopian convent on the roof of the Church.

Return through the market to the Damascus Gate.

VIA DOLOROSA ✪✪✪

The supposed path of Christ's last journey, known as the Via Dolorosa ('Sorrowful Road'), was only institutionalised in the late Middle Ages and passes through a tangle of back streets and alleyways that are now filled with kitsch souvenir stores. The way comprises 14 Stations of the Cross, beginning in the Muslim Quarter near St Stephen's Gate at the Franciscan Complex, which contains the Church of the Condemnation and the Church of the Flagellation. Near by is the Ecce Homo Convent, beneath which is the Lithostratos, the original Roman paving stones upon which Christ may have trodden as he bore the cross. After winding through the main Arab market the Via Dolorosa reaches the Church of the Holy Sepulchre (➤ 31), which contains the final five Stations.

- ✚ 35F4
- ⏱ Lithostratos: daily 8–12, 2–4
- 🚌 1, 99 (St Stephen's Gate)
- ♿ Good
- ❓ Every Fri at 3PM the Franciscan friars lead a procession from the first Station of the Cross

WESTERN WALL ✪✪✪

The original retaining wall of the Temple Mount was left standing by the Romans, it is believed to symbolise their power over the vanquished Jews. As the only remnant of the Temple complex, the Western Wall is considered the holiest shrine in Judaism. The 18m-high stone wall is divided into separate sections for male and female worshippers, who come to put notes and prayers into the wall's cracks in the belief that this is as close as man can come to God. It is also traditional for Jews from around the world to bring their sons here for their *bar mitzvah*, the Jewish ceremony to proclaim a boy passing into manhood. Much of the men's section extends underground to the left of the Wall.

- ✚ 35F3
- 🍴 Near by (£)
- 🚌 1, 38
- ♿ Excellent
- 🚫 Free
- ❓ Photography prohibited on Fri evening, Sat & festivals

Hasidic Jews in prayer at the Western (Wailing) Wall

Did you know ?

You can fax the Western Wall courtesy of the Bezeq Israel Telecommunication Corporation, whose representative will take your prayer and insert it in the wall. The number is (02) 561 2222. Or e-mail from internet site www.thewall.org

 34A1
Ha-Zikaron Street, Mount Herzl
 (02) 644 3400
Sun–Thu 9–4:45, Fri 9–2. Closed Sat and festivals
Café (£)
13, 17, 18, 20, 21, 23, 27, 99
Excellent
Free

Above: *the names of the concentration camps are etched on the black floor of Yad Vashem's Hall of Remembrance*

YAD VASHEM HOLOCAUST MEMORIAL AND MUSEUM

The museum narrates the rise of Nazism and its anti-Semitic policies, which culminated in the Holocaust. It is difficult to digest the clinically efficient cruelty inflicted on the Jewish people by Nazi Germany that this collection of documented evidence and symbolic memorials depicts. The principal memorial is the Hall of Remembrance, a large, empty chamber where an eternal flame burns in front of a vault of victims' ashes. Elsewhere in the complex is a memorial of light to the 1½ million children slaughtered by the Nazis, and an extraordinary exhibition of art from concentration camp inmates, many of them the naively optimistic drawings of children. The Hall of Names contains the names of some four million (so far) of the six million Holocaust victims, inscribed on small plaques. Outside, in the Valley of the Lost Communities, the names of hundreds of decimated Jewish villages are carved into the mountainside.

35D2
Sederot Blumfield

Montefiore Museum
Sun–Thu 9–4, Fri 9–1. Closed Sat
Mishkenot Sha'ananim restaurant (£££)
4, 5, 6, 7, 8, 14, 18, 21, 48
None

YEMIN MOSHE

This charming 19th-century neighbourhood includes Mishkenot Sha'ananim, the first Jewish settlement outside the Old City and today an artists' guest house. Yemin Moshe had degenerated into slum dwellings by the time of the city's reunification in 1967, but since then has become the site of Jerusalem's most expensive real estate. The windmill in the heart of the complex contains the **Montefiore Museum**, an exhibition documenting the history of the quarter, which was built with funds from British philanthropist Moses Montefiore. The stagecoach on display is a reconstruction of the original, burnt in the 1980s, which brought Montefiore to the Holy Land.

Revered since Crusader times as the birthplace of John the Baptist, 'En Kerem now attracts Jerusalem's elite

What to See around Jerusalem

BETHLEHEM (➤ 17, TOP TEN)

'EN KEREM   ✪✪✪

This picturesque village nestles amid grapevines and olive groves in the hills west of Jerusalem, and has become an expensive and fashionable suburb whilst remaining steeped in Christian religious history. Christians believe that John the Baptist was born in 'En Kerem, and that it was here that the Archangel Gabriel told Mary that she would bear the Messiah.

The grotto beneath the Franciscan Church of John the Baptist is allegedly the site of the disciple's birth, while the nearby Church of the Visitation, also Franciscan, is where Mary received the news.

Several kilometres west of the village centre is the Hadassah Medical Centre. The synagogue in the middle of the complex contains the **Chagall Windows**. These heavily stylised and richly coloured stained-glass windows depict the 12 tribes of Israel and are the work of the Jewish artist Marc Chagall.

✚ 47A1
🍴 Cafés (£), restaurants (£££)
🚌 17

Chagall Windows
✉ Hadassah Medical Centre synagogue
🕐 Sun–Thu 8–1:15, 2–3:45, Fri 8–12:45. Closed Sat
🚌 19, 27
♿ Very good
🎫 Free

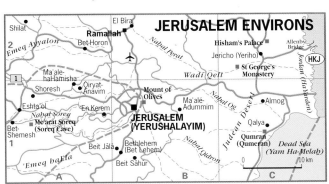

47C2

Many restaurants near by (£)

Hisham's Palace

Qasr Hisham Street

Apr–Oct, daily 8–5;
Nov–Mar, daily 8–4

No public transport from Jerusalem – take a taxi

Good

Moderate

Above: the remains of Hisham's Palace include massive columns and intricate stonework

JERICHO (YERIHO) ✪✪✪

Jericho is an oasis in the desert, lying 270m below sea level and pleasantly warm in winter. Located some 30km east of Jerusalem, Jericho advertises itself as the 'world's oldest known town' because of its 9,000-year-old fortifications. It is also in one of the world's newest states, though strictly speaking Palestine is a collection of autonomous zones rather than a country, and tourists can enter without even having to show a passport.

Ancient Jericho, or Tel Jericho, to the north of the city, shows some unremarkable remains, including some wooden fortifications. What is remarkable is that these remains have been found through carbon-dating to be 10,000 years old. Above the Tel is the Greek Orthodox Monastery of the Temptation (Quarantel) which affords glorious views of Jericho and is supposedly the site where Satan tempted Christ with domain over all he saw. **Hisham's Palace** to the north of the city was the winter retreat of the Islamic leader Hisham, the tenth Umayyad caliph. The palace was destroyed by an earthquake soon after it was built, but the remaining 8th-century ruins include exceptionally well-preserved mosaics. The nearby Shalom Al Yisrael synagogue has a 5th-century mosaic in its cellar.

SOREQ CAVE ✪✪

Set amid the attractive hills and forests of the Soreq Valley, the cave itself is located 19km southwest of Jerusalem and is estimated to be 25 million years old. It was inadvertently discovered in 1968 when the hills were dynamited for quarrying. Beautiful stalagmites and stalactites and other rare geological formations are shown to best advantage by colourful lighting and strategically placed walkways. The countryside around is excellent for hiking.

✚ 47A1
☎ (02) 991 1117
🕐 Sat–Thu 8–3, Fri and eve of festivals 8:30–1. Closed Yom Kippur
🍴 Café (£)
♿ Few (book in advance)
💷 Moderate
❓ Photography on Fri only

WADI QELT ✪✪

Wadi Qelt is a deep, dramatic gorge that cuts an attractive green swathe through the rocks of the Judean Desert. The wadi (dry bed of a torrent) stretches from north of Jerusalem down to Jericho and several springs en route mean that water runs through the wadi throughout the year. This is magnificent hiking country and it is possible to walk the whole 20km length of the wadi; however, the weather is blisteringly hot for most of the year. There is an additional but remote danger of terrorism because the wadi passes through the heart of the West Bank, so do not hike in very small groups. The best place to sample the flavour of the area is at **St George's Monastery**, midway along the wadi. The monastery, clinging precariously to the side of the cliff, is accessible from a path leading down from the old Roman road linking Jerusalem and Jericho.

✚ 47B2

St George's Monastery
🕐 Mon–Sat 8–5. Closed Sun
🍴 None
🚖 Taxi or tour bus only
♿ None
💷 Free

St George's Monastery seems to hang from the rock face

Galilee & the North

This region has some of Israel's most attractive countryside. The windswept beaches north of Haifa are among the country's quietest, while the rolling green hills of the Galilee have a charm that is accentuated by the region's rich religious history. It was here that Christ spent most of his life, and the sacred Jewish texts of the *Mishnah* and the *Kabbalah* were compiled. Indeed, religion seems to have exaggerated the Galilee's scale. The Sea of Galilee is only a small lake, the River Jordan a broad stream, and the entire region is no bigger than Greater London or Los Angeles County.

The terrain is more dramatic further east. Across from the Jordan Rift Valley are the Golan Heights and majestic Mount Hermon, rising to 2,224m (2,766m in Syria). Getting around this essentially rural region by public transport is cumbersome, so a hire car or organised tour are recommended.

' A Land that flowed with Milke and Honey: in the middest as it were of the habitable World, and under a temperate Clime. '

GEORGE SANDYS
Purchas his Pilgrimes, 1610

Basilica of the Annunciation, Nazareth

Haifa (Hefa)

Haifa, Israel's third largest city, is a contrasting mixture of heavy industry and spectacular Mediterranean panoramas. Over 500,000 people live in Haifa and the northern 'Krayot' suburbs, including a large Arab minority and members of the Baha'i faith (▶ 53). Haifa's Jewish majority is stridently secular and there is very little of religious significance in the region. The one exception is Elijah's Cave near the southern entrance to the city, where the prophet allegedly hid from King Ahab after slaughtering the idolatrous priests.

Built on a mountain slope jutting out into the Mediterranean, Haifa is famous for its views

Haifa is built on the slopes of Mount Carmel, and is divided into three tiers; the downtown port, the midtown Hadar commercial district and uptown Central Carmel, where the hotels and views are to be found. The three districts are linked by the Carmelit subway, which is in fact an underground cable car. Haifa's bustling port and the smoke-belching factories stretching north of the city do not detract from the enchanting views to be had from the top of Mount Carmel.

Haifa has two universities, the Technion, one of Israel's most prestigious science institutions, and Haifa University – a high-rise building that stands out on the peak of Mount Carmel. On a clear winter's day the view from the 25th floor stretches northwards to Mount Hermon and southwards past Tel Aviv. To the east and south of the city is the Carmel National Park, where deer and other animals have been successfully reintroduced. When travelling through these hillside forests the visitor is every so often treated to a glorious glimpse of the Mediterranean shimmering in the sun.

BAHA'I SHRINE, WORLD CENTRE AND GARDENS ✪✪

The gold-domed Baha'i Shrine was built early this century to house the bones of Mirza Ali Mohammed, who foreshadowed the Baha'i religion in Persia in 1844 when he proclaimed the coming of a 'promised one'. Mirza Ali Mohammed was executed for heresy in 1850 and his disciples brought his remains to Haifa in 1909. The 'promised one,' Baha'u'llah, the founder of the religion, is actually buried just north of 'Akko. Today there are an estimated three million Baha'is worldwide living mainly in Iran and the US. An offshoot of Islam, the Baha'i faith has an internationalist philosophy, believing that Moses, Christ, Mohammed and Buddha were all messengers of God ('Divine Educators').

Near by is the Baha'i Universal House of Justice (not open to the public), the religion's world headquarters built in the style of the Parthenon on the Acropolis in Athens. The surrounding gardens are said to be the world's longest hillside garden.

➕ 56A3
✉ Ha-Ziyyonat Avenue
☎ (04) 835 8358
🕐 Daily 9–12; gardens until 5
🍴 Opposite entrance (££)
♿ Good
🚌 22, 23, 25, 26, 32
🎟 Free

Above: the elegant Baha'i Shrine inspires quiet worship in a busy city

ISRAEL NATIONAL MUSEUM OF SCIENCE ✪
(AND HAIFA'S OTHER MUSEUMS)

This hands-on science museum is great fun for children and is delightfully located in an attractive oriental-style building in midtown Hadar. This building began life in 1924 as the original Technion, Israel's oldest university.

Other museums worth visiting include the nearby Haifa Museum (ancient and modern art, folklore and ethnography), the Reuben and Edith Hecht Museum (history) at Haifa University, the National Maritime Museum and Illegal Immigration Museum near the Central Bus Station and the Tikotin Museum of Japanese Art in Central Carmel.

➕ 56A3
Science Museum
✉ Balfour Street
☎ (04) 862 8111
🕐 Sun, Mon, Wed, Thu 9–6, Tue 9–7:30, Fri 10–3, Sat 10–5
🍴 Café (£)
🚇 Carmelit: Hanevi'im Station
♿ Good
🎟 Moderate

From Haifa to Upper Galilee

Distance
210km

Time
5 hours without stops, 8
hours with stops

Start point
Haifa
✚ 56A3

End point
Mount Tabor
✚ 56B2

Lunch
Hakfar Restaurant (The
Village) (££)
✉ Rosh-Pinna, near the bus
station
☎ (06) 693 8026

*Head north from Haifa on Highway 4, passing
through the heavily industrialised northern
suburbs.*

The Mediterranean coast from the ancient port of 'Akko
(► 16) northwards offers some of the country's most
deserted beaches, save for the resort of Nahariya. Try
taking a dip at Akhziv, just south of the Lebanese border at
Rosh HaNikra.

*One kilometre south of Rosh HaNikra turn
right and travel eastwards along Route 899.*

Known as the Northern Road, this highway straddles the
Lebanese border and passes through dramatic hillside
scenery. The landscape can be viewed from Montfort,
10km along the highway, a castle fortress built by the
Crusaders in 1226.

*Route 899 eventually descends into the Hula
Valley, 9km north of the Hula Nature Reserve
(► 59).*

The Upper Galilee town of Rosh-Pinna, to the south, was
the first Jewish town to be set up after Roman times.
Established in 1880, the town retains its rustic charm and
makes an excellent stopping point for lunch.

*The Franciscan Basilica of
the Transfiguration on
Mount Tabor*

*Continue south along Highway 90. Turn right
after several kilometres (westwards) along
Highway 85 and after 7km turn left
(southwards) on to Highway 65. After
30km Mount Tabor is on your right and
the summit can be reached via the Arab
village of Daburiya.*

Mount Tabor, looking like a large hump,
combines religious history with a marvellous
view from its peak. From here history says that
the prophetess Deborah led her army to
vanquish the idol-worshipping Canaanites in the
12th century BC, and it was here that Jesus
Christ appeared after his death to Peter, James and John,
his face shining 'like the sun' and in pure white raiment.

*Return on Highway 65 via 'Afula to Hadera and
then back to Haifa or Tel Aviv.*

'AKKO (► 16, TOP TEN)

BEIT SHE'AN ⭐⭐

Located in the Jordan Valley 120m below sea level, this is at first glance a dusty, ugly town. However, it was once a great city – a member of the Decapolis, the 10 most important Eastern Mediterranean cities during Roman times. Standing at the strategic meeting point between the Jordan and Jezreel Valleys, Beit She'an has been settled for over 5,000 years and is mentioned in Egyptian texts from 4,000 years ago as well as in the book of Samuel. Archaeological excavations at Tel Beit She'an have revealed finds from both these periods. But it is the Roman and Byzantine remains that are most worth seeing. These include Israel's best-preserved amphitheatre with seating for 8,000 spectators, and a 2nd-century temple and colonnaded street lined with stores.

➕ 57C1
🕐 Apr–Oct, Sat–Thu 8–5, Fri 8–4; Nov–Mar, Sat–Thu 8–4, Fri 8–3
🍴 Near by (£)
🚍 961, 963 (Jerusalem)
♿ Good
✋ Moderate

CAESAREA ⭐⭐⭐

This ancient Phoenician settlement (founded c400 BC) is situated on the coast midway between Tel Aviv and Haifa. Herod rebuilt it as a new city in honour of the Roman emperor Augustus, with a harbour that was one of the great engineering feats of its age. After the Arabs captured the city in AD 637 the harbour silted up and Caesarea declined until the 11th-century Crusader conquest. The Crusaders restored the port and Caesarea once again prospered until their defeat in 1251 by the Asiatic warriors known as Mamelukes, who eventually destroyed the city.

The Crusader city in Caesarea includes a church, houses and an arcaded street as well as some Byzantine excavations. To the south, the Roman amphitheatre, with its backdrop of the sea, is a delightful place to take in a concert. There is also a restored hippodrome and sections of a 16km aqueduct run along Caesarea's golden beach, much of it buried beneath the sand.

➕ 56A1
☎ (06) 636 1358
🕐 Sat, Mon–Thu 8–4, Fri 8–3. Closed Sun
🍴 By the site (£)
🚍 72 (from Hadera); 852, 872 (to Hadera from Tel Aviv or Haifa); 947 (to Hadera from Jerusalem)
♿ Good
✋ Moderate
❓ Enquire at theatre agencies about any upcoming concerts at the amphitheatre

Ceasarea's ancient aqueduct is an unusual backdrop for a beach picnic

Modern sculpture on the seafront at Caesarea

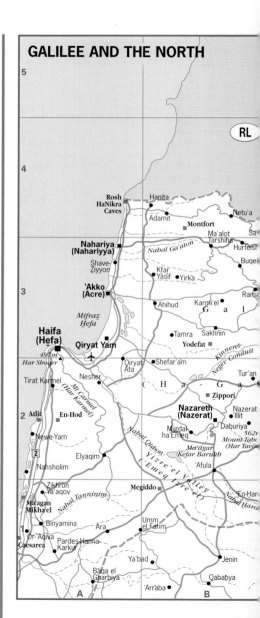

GALILEE AND THE NORTH

RL

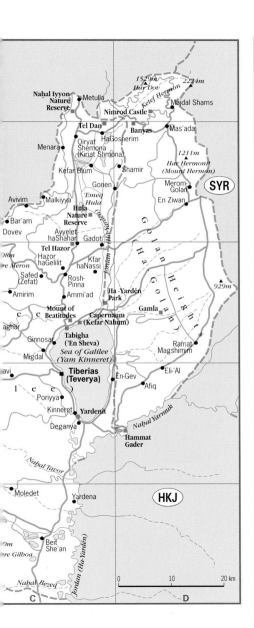

1529m
Har Dov
2224m

Nahal Iyyon Nature Reserve ■Metulla
Ketef Hermon ■Majdal Shams
Nimrod Castle ■
Tel Dan ■
HaGosherim
Banyas ■Mas'ada
Menara• Qiryat Shemona (Kiriat Shmona)
1211m
Har Hermonit (Mount Hermon) ▲
Kefar Blum ■Shamir
Gonen•
'Emeq Hula
Merom-Golan•
Avivim• Malkiyya•
Hula Nature Reserve
En Ziwan•
(SYR)
•Bar'am
Dovev•
Ayyelet haShahar■ Gadot•
•08m *re Meron*
Tel Hazor ■
Hazor haGelilit•
Kfar haNassi•
Safed (Zefat)•
Rosh-Pinna•
•Amirim
Ammi'ad•
Ha-Yarden Park ■
929m ▲
Mount of Beatitudes ■
Capernaum (Kefar Nahum) ■
Gamla•
•e e •aghar
Ginnosar•
Tabigha ('En Sheva) ■
Sea of Galilee (Yam Kinneret)
Ramat Magshimim•
Migdal•
•avi
Tiberias (Teverya)
En-Gev•
•Eli-'Al
•l e e
Poriyya•
Afiq•
Kinneret• **Yardenit** ■
Nahal Yarmuk
Deganya•
Hammat Gader ■
Nahal Tavor
•Moledet
Yardena•
(HKJ)
•0m *re Gilboa*
Beit She'an•
Jordan (Ha Yarden)
Nahal Bezeq
0   10   20 km
C   D

Best catch of the day on the Sea of Galilee

57

57C3
Daily 8:30–4:15
Near by (££)
941, 963 (walk eastwards on highway 87 from the Kefar Nahum junction)
Good
Cheap

Striking marble columns once supported Capernaum's ancient synagogue

CAPERNAUM (KEFAR NAHUM)

This idyllic spot on the northern shore of the Sea of Galilee was Christ's home for a period, and it is said that he preached more sermons and performed more miracles here than in any other place. It was here that he healed the centurion's servant, Peter's stepmother, the paralytic and others as recounted in the gospels. Five of Christ's disciples, including Peter, are said to have come from Capernaum. Neglected over the centuries, the Franciscans acquired the entire site in 1894. They have partly restored a 2nd-century synagogue believed to be built over a more ancient one where Christ himself preached. A church shaped like a ship has been built here, completed in 1990. The finds from the archaeological excavations on the site are also on show, including ruins from a 13th-century BC settlement; the finds indicate this was a flourishing town until Byzantine times.

GOLAN HEIGHTS (HA-GOLAN) ✪✪

The black volcanic rocks of the Golan Heights rise over a 1,000m to the east of the Galilee and stretch northwards 60km to the foothills of Mount Hermon. These strategically crucial hills were captured by Israel from Syria in 1967 and have been jealously contested since. Sights worth visiting in the region include **Nimrod Castle**, a 12th-century Crusader castle with a commanding view, and the Ram Pool, peculiarly located in an extinct volcano. Both sights are in the north near the Druze village of Mas'ada. In the south of the region are Gamla, the site of an important Roman victory over Jewish rebels, and the **Hammat Gader** hot springs, which feature an alligator enclosure as well as Roman ruins and a modern bath complex.

HULA VALLEY ('EMEQ HULA) ✪✪

Until the 1950s the Hula Valley, located north of the Sea of Galilee, was a mosquito-infested swamp. The draining of the Hula Valley eradicated malaria and transformed the marshlands into fertile, farming land. This was hailed as one of Israel's great achievements but by the 1980s the excessive amount of peat in the soil was making the land difficult to farm. In an ambitious project, much of the land is now being reflooded. The destroyed ecosystem can never be fully restored but the **Hula Nature Reserve** offers a fascinating tour through 80 hectares of swamps that were preserved when the area was drained in 1956. An hour-long stroll enables the visitor to observe herons, egrets, moorhens and warblers nesting among the world's most northerly papyrus thickets, as well as the star attraction – water buffalo.

✚ 57D3

Nimrod Castle
✚ 57D5
⊘ Apr–Sep, Mon–Sat 8–5;
Oct–Mar Mon–Sat 8–4.
Closed Sun
🖐 Cheap

Hammat Gader
✚ 57D2
⊘ Mon–Thu 8am–9:30pm,
Fri 8am–11:30pm, Sat
8–8, Sun 8–4:30
🖐 Expensive

✚ 57C4

Hula Nature Reserve
☎ (04) 693 7069
⊘ Apr–Oct, daily 8–4;
Nov–Mar, daily 8–3
🍴 Café (£)
♿ Excellent
🖐 Moderate

---

*Above: Nimrod Castle,
scene of many battles*

59

57C3

? For more details of
  watersports on the River
  Jordan ➤ 115

Below: *resting by the cool
waters of the Banyas
river*

JORDAN RIVER (HA-YARDÉN) ●●●

Though one of the world's most famous rivers, the Jordan is but a broad stream. Three tributaries descending from Mount Hermon – the Banyas, Dan and Hasban – meet up at almost the same point near Kibbutz Sde Nehemya east of Kiriat Shmona. The river then flows 265km southwards through the Galilee and the Sea of Galilee and on via the Jordan Valley to the Dead Sea. It is possible to float down the river on a variety of craft including inner-tubes, kayaks and katarafts (➤ 43) and there is a baptismal site near Kibbutz Deganya, where the river flows out of the Sea of Galilee.

Did you know ?

There are three bridges across the river linking Israel and Jordan. The Sheikh Hussein Bridge near Beit She'an was only opened after the peace treaty in 1994. But even when Israel and Jordan were officially at war several hundred thousand people annually would cross the Allenby Bridge near Jericho and the Adam Bridge further north.

 56B1

✉ North of Megiddo
  Junction, Hadera–'Afula
  highway

☎ (04) 652 2167

🕐 Apr–Sep, Sat–Thu 8–4:45,
  Fri 8–3:45; Oct–Mar,
  Sat–Thu 8–3:45, Fri
  8–2:45

🍴 Café (£)

♿ Few

💲 Moderate

MEGIDDO ✪

Megiddo is a fortified hill overlooking a narrow pass that was once part of the supply and trade route between Egypt and Syria. Because of its strategic position it has been much fought over: Pharaoh Thutmose III of Egypt won a glorious victory here in 1478 BC, while in 610 BC the Israelite king Josiah was killed here. Britain's General Allenby won the crucial World War I battle at Megiddo that resulted in control of Palestine passing from the Turks to the British. Israeli and Arab forces clashed here in 1948. According to the Book of Revelations, even Armageddon, 'the final battle', will be fought here.

Local excavations have revealed 20 layers of civilisation, including a 4,000-year-old Canaanite temple, and an underground water system from the time of King Ahab in 800 BC.

Along the Northern Shore of the Sea of Galilee

You don't have to be a Christian to enjoy this walk even though it covers one of the most important clusters of sites in Christendom. Sprituality aside, the sweeping scenic views of distant mountains and the serenity of the lake stimulate the senses, while any curious intellect is fascinated by the region where Christ spent important years of his life.

Begin at the Mount of the Beatitudes (➤ 62). From the Franciscan church there is a track leading down to Tabigha (➤ 63). Several tracks lead off in different directions, so make for the two churches at Tabigha, the church to the left built from distinctive black rock.

In spring the hillside is ablaze with flowers. At Tabigha, aside from the Church of the Multiplication of the Loaves and Fishes, the Church of the Primacy of St Peter is also worth investigating; it is built from the local black basalt rock. There are also some attractive small springs in the vicinity.

Walk eastwards towards Capernaum. The Kfar Nahum restaurant by the ancient settlement is a good place for lunch; appropriately it is a fish restaurant, specialising in the local St Peter's fish.

Just north of Capernaum is a red-roofed Greek Orthodox monastery, while several kilometres further along is Amnun Beach, a good place to take a dip; slightly further on still the road passes over the River Jordan. Just to the south the river flows into the lake, while to the north is Ha-Yardén Park, which has the river as its centrepiece. You can hire a kayak here and go for a paddle.

Distance
9km

Time
Several hours, but half a day with stops at the churches

Start point
Mount of the Beatitudes
57C3
941, 963 (from Tiberias)

End point
Ha-Yardén Park
57C3
16, 19 (from Tiberias)

Lunch
Kfar Nahum Restaurant
D N Korazim, Kfar Nahum
(04) 672 4805.

Greek Orthodox monastery, Capernaum

METULLA

Founded in 1896 by European Jews, Metulla feels more Alpine than Middle Eastern. The Swiss-like tranquillity is odd considering that the town is surrounded by Lebanon on three sides. At an elevation of 525m the air is fresh even in the heat of the summer and the town has a number of charming small hotels and an ice-skating rink. The 'Good Fence' border crossing north of the town has a lookout point over Israel's troubled northern neighbour.

Church of the Beatitudes

MOUNT OF THE BEATITUDES

This is believed to be the hill where Christ preached the Sermon on the Mount. The site is owned by the Franciscans, who constructed an attractive octagonal church (representing the eight beatitudes – the types of people who will be rewarded in heaven) now used by Italian nuns who live in an adjacent hospice. From the circular gallery of the convent there is a good view of the Sea of Galilee, and on the hillside there are remains of a 4th-century chapel.

MOUNT HERMON (HAR HERMONIT)

The Hermon range is 45km long and 25km wide, and dominates its surroundings, with peaks in Israel, Lebanon and Syria. Its highest summit of 2,766m is located in Lebanon while the highest Israeli-held peak of 2,224m was captured from Syria in 1967. This strategic summit, a closed military zone, has a commanding view of Damascus just 50km to the northeast. However, visitors do have access to the modest ski slope just beneath the Israeli-held summit, depending on seasonal snowfalls.

NAZARETH (► 24, TOP TEN)

ROSH HANIKRA CAVES ✪

This fascinating underground network of caves is at the northernmost point on Israel's Mediterranean coast, by the Israel-Lebanon border crossing point. Carved out by the sea, the caves can only be reached by a cable-car descending the rugged cliffs. Swimming is strictly prohibited because bathers risk inadvertently returning to the shore on the wrong side of the border.

SAFED (➤ 25, TOP TEN)

SEA OF GALILEE (➤ 26, TOP TEN)

TABIGHA ('EN SHEVA) ✪✪

It is here that Christ is believed to have performed the miracle of the fishes and loaves, feeding 5,000 people with just two fishes and five loaves. Close to Capernaum on the northern shore of the Sea of Galilee, this idyllic area is known in Greek as *Heptapegon* because of the seven springs that flow into the lake here. The site was later abandoned until 1932, when a German archaeologist discovered some mosaic floors, including a symbolic mosaic representation of two fishes and a loaf. Over the site of a 5th-century Byzantine basilica German Catholics completed the Byzantine-style stone-faced **Church of the Multiplication of the Loaves and Fishes** in 1982. A Benedictine monastery stands near the church and just to the north is the Church of the Primacy of St Peter, where Christ allegedly appeared for a third time after the resurrection and asserted St Peter's supremacy.

TIBERIAS (TEVERYA) ✪✪

Established in AD 20 by Herod Antipas as a health resort because of its hot springs, the city was named after the Roman emperor Tiberius. During the second century Tiberias was the centre of Jewish scholarship, and it was here that the part of the Talmud Jewish scriptures, known as the *Mishnah* (oral law), was compiled. Ancient Tiberias was destroyed by a 19th-century earthquake, and the modern city is bustling and unexceptional.

✚ 56A4
🕐 Oct–Mar daily 8:30–4 (to 11PM Jul & Aug); Apr–Sep Sat–Thu 8:30–6, Fri 8:30–4
🍴 Restaurant (££)
♿ None
💰 Moderate

Above: *down to the caves at Rosh HaNikra*

✚ 57C3
🍴 Restaurant (££)
🚌 941, 963 from Tiberias

Church of the Multiplication of the Loaves and Fishes
🕐 Mon–Sat 8:30–5, Sun 9:15–5
♿ Excellent
✋ Free

✚ 57C2
🍴 Try the lakeside fish restaurants in the centre of town (££)
🚌 961 (from Jerusalem)

Tel Aviv & the Central Region

Dominated by Tel Aviv-Yafo and its suburbs, this densely populated region comprises the heart of modern Israel. Greater Tel Aviv – reaching to Kfar Saba in the northeast, Rishon le-Ziyyon in the southeast and Bat Yam in the south – has nearly 2.5 million residents. The coastal plain – one long golden beach – stretches from Ashkelon in the south, where Samson brought down the house on his Philistine captors, to Jaffa and Tel Aviv itself. To the north are the exclusive resort of Herzliyya and for the more budget conscious, Netanya. This region is predominantly secular, with the exception of Tel Aviv's ultra-orthodox suburb of Bnei Braq.

The coastal plain, although densely populated by modern Israelis, was not the domain of the ancient Israelites. In biblical times it was the Philistines who controlled the coast while the Israelites lived on the inland hills. Today those hills are the location of the Palestinian West Bank, known as Judea and Samaria to the Jews.

> ‘ *[its] planning and architecture,*
> *its smiling communal life, its*
> *intellectual pursuits and its air of*
> *youth enthroned ... are all an*
> *accomplished fact.* ’
>
> ROBERT BYRON on Tel Aviv
> *The Road to Oxiana* (1937)

High-rise hotels, Tel Aviv

Tel Aviv

Describing itself as the city that never stops, Tel Aviv is a young city with a young soul. It was founded in 1909 north of the ancient city of Jaffa and grew rapidly in the 1920s, establishing itself as the quintessential modern Jewish city. If Jerusalem symbolised the glory of the Jewish past, then Tel Aviv quickly came to represent the promise of a more prosperous future. Tel Aviv is hedonistic and materialistic but also prides itself on its culture – its museums, theatres, orchestras and art galleries. It is undoubtedly the country's commercial capital and vies with Jerusalem over being the principle cultural centre.

It is unquestionably the leisure capital, too. Dizengoff, once the city's most fashionable thoroughfare for stores and cafés, has now been eclipsed by other attractions. Shenkin, near the financial district, is the city's trendiest neighbourhood, while Florentine is even more Bohemian. The Carmel Market is the place for bargains, and nearby Nahalat Binyamin Street has pleasant streetside cafés. However, for visitors the seaside promenade stretching from the restaurant district in Little Old Tel Aviv all the way south to Jaffa is the place to head for. Try the restaurants in the Yemenite Quarter and stroll through the gentrified streets of Neve Tzedek. North Tel Aviv, on the far side of the River Yarkon around the campus of Tel Aviv University, is where the city's most salubrious suburbs are found, while south of the city, around the Central Bus Station, are the seedier, more impoverished quarters.

Its outdoor tables and exuberant street life identify Tel Aviv as a Mediterranean city

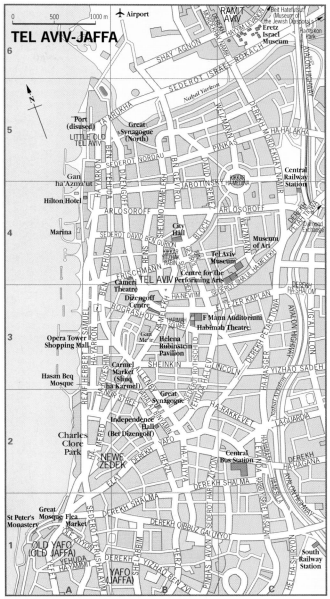

TEL AVIV-JAFFA

✈ Airport

0   500   1000 m

RAMIT
AVIV

Beit Hatefutsot
(Museum of
the Jewish Diaspora)

Eretz
Israel
Museum

Hayarkon
Park

SHAY AGNON

SEDEROT ISRAEL ROKACH

Nahal Yarkon

Port
(disused)
LITTLE OLD
TEL AVIV

Great
Synagogue
(North)

DEREKH MORDEKHAI NAMIR

HAYIM LEVANON

DEREKH NAMIR

AVALON HIGHWAY

WEIZMANN

HA-HALAKHA

N

SEDEROT NORDAU

PINKAS

Gan
ha'Azma'ut

JABOTINSKY

KIKKAR
HA-MEDINA

Central
Railway
Station

Hilton Hotel

ARLOSOROFF

ARLOSOROFF

DEREKH PETAH-TIQWA

Diamond
Exchange

Marina

SEDEROT DAVID BEN-GURION

City
Hall

KIKKAR
YITZHAK
RABIN

BLOCH

Tel Aviv
Museum

Museum
of Art

Centre for the
Performing Arts

Cameri
Theatre

TEL AVIV

SEDEROT SHAUL HAMELEKH

DEREKH
HA-SHALOM

Dizengoff
Centre

HA-NEVI'IM

ELIEZER KAPLAN

BOGRASHOV

HABIMAH-
SQUARE

F Mann Auditorium

Habimah Theatre

AVALON HIGHWAY

YIGAL ALLON

Opera Tower
Shopping Mall

Gan
Me'ir

Helena
Rubinstein
Pavilion

HA-MASGER

YIZHAQ SADEH

Carmel
Market
(Shuq
ha'Karmel)

SHEINKIN

LINCOLN

Hasan Beq
Mosque

NUR STREET

Great
Synagogue

YEHUDA HALEVI

HA-RAKKEVET

LA GUARDIA

Independence
Hall
(Bet Dizengoff)

Charles
Clore
Park

NEWE
ZEDEK

YAFO

HERZL

HA-ALIYA

Central
Bus Station

DEREKH
HA-HAGANA

AVALON HIGHWAY

DEREKH SHALMA

St Peter's
Monastery

Great
Mosque Flea
Market

DEREKH SHALMA

SEDEROT YERUSHALAYIM

DEREKH QIBBUZ GALUYYOT

South
Railway
Station

OLD YAFO
(OLD JAFFA)

YEHUDA
HA-YAMMIT

DEREKH
LABBIM

YIZHAQ BEN ZVI

YAFO
(JAFFA)

PINHAS LAVON

A   B   C

67

67C4
1 Jabotinsky Street, Ramat Gan
cafés and restaurants (£–£££)
23, 51, 68, 69

Harry Oppenheimer Diamond Museum
(03) 576 0219
Sun–Thu 10–4, Tue 10–5. Closed Fri, Sat and festivals
Good
Cheap

DIAMOND EXCHANGE

Israel is the world's largest exporter of cut and polished diamonds with annual sales of over $6 billion. Located to the east of the Ayalon Highway, the main traffic artery running through Tel Aviv, in the suburb of Ramat Gan is the Diamond and Precious Stones Exchange. This complex and the surrounding cluster of gleaming high-rise buildings form one of the country's commercial nerve centres. Within the Diamond Exchange is the **Harry Oppenheimer Diamond Museum**, which attractively and intelligently presents the story behind these precious stones.

Byzantine mosaic from western Galilee on display in the Eretz Israel Museum

67C6
2 Haim Levanon Street, Ramat Aviv
(03) 641 5244
Sun–Thu 9–3 (Wed until 5), Fri, Sat and festivals 10–2
Café (£)
25
Excellent
Moderate
Walks (in English) every Sat at 11AM from main entrance

ERETZ ISRAEL MUSEUM

The Land of Israel Museum is located around the excavations of Tel Qasile, a settlement mound with evidence of 12 layers of civilisation dating back to the 12th century BC. There are also remnants of three Philistine temples from that period. Eleven pavilions encircling the site contain exhibitions on, among others, glass, ceramics, coins, ancient tools, folklore and ethnography and the history of the alphabet. The most recently added Landscapes of The Holy Land Park recreates the way farmers tilled the land in biblical times. An imaginative mix of artefacts and models makes this an absorbing museum, bringing archaeology and anthropology to life and offering the visitor a comprehensive understanding of the history of the region.

Did you know ?

The name Tel Aviv is mentioned in the book of Ezekiel as a town in Babylon. Tel Aviv's founders chose the name because of its old-new connotations. Tel is a hill comprising layers of ancient civilisations, while Aviv is Hebrew for spring, the season of renewal.

Along Tel Aviv's Seafront Promenade

Start at Little Old Tel Aviv to the north of the city centre.

In fact there is no access to the seafront from Little Old Tel Aviv, a neighbourhood of fashionable restaurants and pubs and expensive but unassuming apartments. Tel Aviv port, now disused, was established here in 1936. Heading south along HaYarkon Street and entering Gan Ha'azmaut, it is possible to enjoy the seafront from these clifftop gardens or descend to the beach itself. At night this park, just north of the Hilton, is a pick-up point for male homosexuals.

South of the Hilton descend to the promenade by Tel Aviv's marina.

Diving equipment can be rented at the marina by qualified divers. This section of the promenade has the city's most popular beaches, which tend to be very busy on a Saturday between April and October. Towering over the promenade are the city's most expensive hotels, but further along, after Opera Tower at the junction of Allenby Street, (famous for its up-market jewellery and souvenir stores), the seafront apartments become seedier although the beach is still powdery white sand.

Distance
5km

Time
3–6 hours depending on stops

Start point
Corner of HaYarkon and Ta'arukha Streets
✚ 67A5
🚌 4

End point
St Peter's Monastery, Jaffa
✚ 67A1
🚌 25, 46, 91

Lunch
Zion Exclusive Restaurant
✉ 28 Peduim Street
☎ (03) 517 8714

At the Hasan Bek Mosque, in the shadow of another cluster of high-rise hotels and office blocks, detour inland along Nur Street and then turn left into the Carmel Market.

All the fresh fruit and vegetables are likely to whet the appetite. On the left of the market are the restaurants of the Yemenite Quarter. Try the modestly priced Zion restaurant. After lunch return to the seafront and continue southwards to Jaffa (► 21).

Appetising local produce for sale at the Carmel Market

67B3
Junction of Bograshov Street and Rothschild Boulevard
Restaurant (££)
5
Excellent

Helena Rubinstein Pavilion
6 Tarsat Boulevard
(03) 528 7196
Sun–Thu 10–6 (Tue until 10PM), Fri and Sat 10–2
Moderate

HABIMAH SQUARE

The complex of cultural institutions by the square is considered the most important in Israel. The Habimah Theatre houses Israel's national theatre company – the Habimah (meaning the stage) which was founded in Russia in 1918 and relocated to Tel Aviv a decade later. Most performances are in Hebrew but simultaneous translations are often available in several languages. The same is true of the Carmeri Theatre in nearby Dizengoff. Adjoining the Habimah is the Mann Auditorium, home of the Israel Philharmonic Orchestra (IPO). Since it was established in 1937, many stars such as Yitzah Perlman, Daniel Barenboim and Pinchas Zucherman have begun their careers with the IPO, conducted by the Indian-born maestro Zubin Mehta. Next door is the **Helena Rubinstein Pavilion**, which puts on exhibitions of contemporary art by Israeli and foreign artists.

67C6
Cafés (£)
25
Excellent
Large open-air concerts are frequently held in the park. Check with ticket agents

Above: *the modern abstract sculpture in front of the Habimah Theatre is a national landmark*

HA-YARKON PARK

A refuge of countryside amid the concrete of Tel Aviv, the park is an expanse of green that accompanies the River Yarkon as it flows eastwards from its estuary just north of the port in Little Old Tel Aviv. The Yarkon once marked the border between the tribes of Dan and Ephraim; today it separates the city proper from its northern suburbs. Though the river is merely a stream, the parklands along the banks have been attractively landscaped. It is also worth exploring the sources of the Yarkon, only 15km inland near Rosh Ha'ayin. In contrast, the river estuary near the Reading Power Station is unappealing; further upstream in Ramat Gan the river is polluted, and there have even been fatalities after people have swallowed large amounts of the river's water. It is possible to hire rowing boats, but beware.

MUSEUM OF THE JEWISH DIASPORA ✪✪✪

The Museum of the Jewish Diaspora (Beit Hatefutsut) tells the story of the Jewish people during two millennia of exile. Located in north Tel Aviv by the campus of Tel Aviv University, the museum was considered innovative when it opened in 1978 because it presented a narrative rather than exhibiting artefacts. The story of how the Jews retained their identity despite persecution and assimilation is told thematically rather than chronologically. Six subjects are presented: family; community; faith; culture; among the nations (devoted to interaction with the non-Jewish environment); and return (focusing on the return to Israel as a factor in Diaspora life). The Museum uses a variety of technological tricks to bring the topic alive including a 'Chronosphere', a planetarium-type hall in which a 30-minute audio-visual display on Jewish world history is presented by 35 synchronised projectors. Visitors with Jewish roots can feed family names into a computer and receive a print-out of their genealogy.

➕ 67C6
✉ Klausner Street, Ramat Aviv
☎ (03) 646 2020
🕐 Sun–Thu 10–4, Wed until 6. Closed Fri, Sat and festivals
🍴 Café (£)
🚌 25
♿ Excellent
💰 Expensive

Above: *mid-17th-century Polish synagogue ceiling at the Museum of the Diaspora*

THE TEL AVIV CENTRE FOR THE PERFORMING ARTS AND MUSEUM OF ART ✪

The Centre for the Performing Arts was opened in 1995; it houses the Israel Opera, and holds regular performances by the Israel Ballet and other dance troupes as well as concerts by the Zion Symphony Orchestra. Adjacent to the centre is the **Tel Aviv Museum of Art**, which is the country's largest museum devoted to the fine arts. In addition to a comprehensive collection of Israeli and Jewish art, paintings by Renoir, Monet, Van Gogh, Picasso and other great artists are on permanent exhibition.

➕ 67C4
🚌 18, 32, 70

Tel Aviv Museum of Art
✉ 27 Sha'ul Ha-Melekh St
☎ (03) 695 7361
🕐 Sun–Thu 10–6 (Wed until 10PM), Fri and Sat 10–2
🍴 Restaurant (££)
♿ Excellent
💰 Moderate

71

Food & Drink

A frequent sight in Israel – an illuminated sign advertising a kosher restaurant

Keeping Kosher

The kosher dietary laws, which almost all hotels and many restaurants in Israel adhere to, are not so much a cooking style as a set of prohibitions and requirements stipulated by Jewish law. Muslim dietary laws are very similar, meaning that Arab-owned restaurants follow a similar code. Pork, ham and bacon are of course forbidden foods, as are seafoods, with the exception of most fish. Meat must be drained of all its blood, making beef less succulent, although imaginative use of seasoning and sauces can compensate for this.

Most significantly, meat (including poultry) must be kept entirely separate from dairy products. So do not expect a cheese board after a steak, or butter with bread, or milk in coffee when eating meat. On the other hand, vegetarians can rest assured that a dairy restaurant is not serving up anything containing meat. This said, many restaurants, especially outside Jerusalem, do not observe kosher dietary laws.

Middle Eastern Cuisine

Everything is available in Israel from Chinese and Italian food to Indian and French cuisine as well as the usual range of internationally known fast food outlets peddling hamburgers, pizzas and fried chicken. Ironically, restaurants serving traditional Eastern European Jewish food are often the most difficult to find. However, it is Middle

Cakes galore on sale in Jerusalem's Old City

Eastern cooking that dominates. The range of appetising *mezze* salads, such as houmous, tahina and tabouleh eaten with pitta bread are excellent, while entrées can be disappointing. Fish is lean though served well seasoned and meat is often desiccated. Meat on skewers, *shipudim*, is the local speciality. Puddings such as *bakhlawe* are delicious if you have a sweet tooth and are not fussy about your calorie intake.

Surly Service

Even in very expensive restaurants service can be most politely described as informal, which can make eating out in a pricey restaurant a disappointment. However, as throughout the Mediterranean, the average standard of cooking is very high and visitors who take their chances and enter any conveniently located restaurant are likely to be pleasantly surprised. Falafel bars offer a very cheap and healthy way of eating, and are usually found near central bus stations; the fried chick-pea balls are generally served in pitta bread with chips and as much salad as you can eat. Hotels lay on wonderfully large buffet breakfasts with fruit, vegetables, cereals, smoked fish and cheeses.

Drinks

Until a decade ago Israeli wines were seen as a joke, but the country's wine industry has now progressed in leaps and bounds, led by the Golan winery. Beer is cold and wet but little more, while local spirit *arak* is a variation of Greek *ouzo*. Generally Israelis do not drink much alcohol and are intolerant of drunkenness.

Coffee is extremely popular. The locals drink Turkish coffee or a similar black brew known affectionately as 'mud', while cappuccino is also a local favourite. Tea is best avoided, though some establishments offer interesting herbal varieties. Best of all are the fresh fruit juices squeezed at streetside cafés. In Jerusalem's Old City try *sahlab*, a sweet, hot and milky drink.

A tempting variety of ethnic dishes are available from street stalls

Wines from the Golan Heights are becoming ever more popular

*Busker in Independence
Square in the centre of
Netanya*

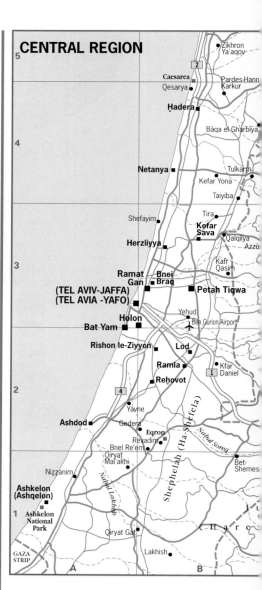

CENTRAL REGION

Zikhron
Ya'aqov

Caesarea
Qesarya

Pardes-Hann
Karkur

Hadera

Bâqa el Gharbīya

Netanya

Tulkarm

Kefar Yona

Taiyiba

Tira

Shefayim

Kefar
Sava

Qalqilya

Azzû

Kafr
Qasim

Herzliyya

Ramat
Gan

Bnei
Braq

Petah Tiqwa

(TEL AVIV-JAFFA)
(TEL AVIA -YAFO)

Yehud

Ben Gurion Airport

Holon

Bat Yam

Rishon le-Ziyyon

Lod

Ramla

Kfar
Daniel

Rehovot

Yavne

Ashdod

Gedera

Eqron

Revadim

Bnei Re'em

Qiryat
Mal'akhi

Nahal Soreq

Bet-
Shemes

Nizzanim

Nahal Lakhish

Shephelah (Ha-Shefela)

Ashkelon
(Ashqelon)

Ashkelon
National
Park

Qiryat Gat

Lakhish

GAZA
STRIP

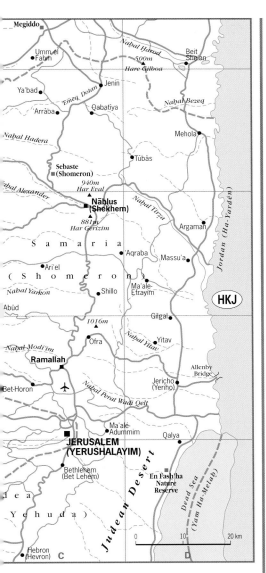

Megiddo

Umm el
Fahm

Nahal Harod

Beit
Shean

500m
Hare Gilboa

Ya'bad

Jenin

Emeq Dotan

Arrāba

Qabatiya

Nahal Bezeq

Nahal Hadera

Mehola

Tūbās

Sebaste
(Shomeron)

940m
Har Eval

Nahal Alexander

**Nāblus
(Shekhem)**

Nahal Tirza

881m
Har Gerizim

Argaman

S a m a r i a

Aqraba

Massu'a

Ari'el

(S h o m e r o n)

Nahal Yarkon

Shillo

Ma'ale-
Efrayim

Abūd

HKJ

1016m

Gilgal

Nahal Yitav

Ofra

Yitav

Nahal Modi'im

Ramallah

Nahal Perat Wadi Qelt

Allenby
Bridge

Bet-Horon

Jericho
(Yeriho)

Ma'ale-
Adummim

**JERUSALEM
(YERUSHALAYIM)**

Qalya

Bethlehem
(Bet Lehem)

**En Fash'ha
Nature
Reserve**

Judean Desert

Jordan (Ha-Yarden)

*Dead Sea
(Yam Ha-Melah)*

d e a

Y e h u d a)

0   10   20 km

Hebron
(Hevron)

C

D

*Samaritan high priest in
Nablus*

Roman statue of Isis with child in Ashkelon National Park

🚩 74A1

Ashkelon National Park
☎ (08) 673 6444
🕐 Apr–Sep, daily 7–7; Oct–Mar, daily 7–4:30
🍴 Cafés and restaurants (£–££)
🚌 438 (from Jerusalem); 300 (from Tel Aviv); 6 (from Ashkelon Bus Station)
🛈 (08) 673 2412
♿ Very good
🅿 Free for visitors on foot; moderate charge for cars

🚩 74B3
🍴 Restaurants (£££)
🚌 90 (from Tel Aviv)
♿ Excellent access to beaches

ASHKELON ✪✪

Ashkelon was one of the Philistines' five principal cities, and it was here that Samson was imprisoned after being betrayed by his wife Delilah. The **National Park**, by the beach, contains remains not only from the Philistine period but also from a 4,000-year-old Canaanite settlement. In addition there are relics from the Greek, Roman, Byzantine and the Crusader periods. The amphitheatre and colonnaded street are Roman, while the walls were built by the Crusaders. Modern Ashkelon, 56km south of Tel Aviv, has undergone rapid development in recent years and, as Israel's southernmost Mediterranean resort before the Gaza Strip, is also popular for its beaches. A new marina was recently completed north of the city, and, if you have a car, try Nitzanim beach, 7km further north of Ashkelon – a palm tree paradise with nearby freshwater pools.

HERZLIYYA ✪

Herzliyya, the expensive resort 15km north of Tel Aviv, is named after Theodore Herzl, the founder of modern political Zionism. The Viennese Herzl would have approved of the high-society image pervading the city that bears his name. The neighbourhood of Herzliyya Pituach, west of the Tel Aviv/Haifa highway, houses many of Tel Aviv's diplomatic corps as well as the elite of Israeli society. Those who thrive on exclusivity will enjoy the costly hotels and the beaches. South of the city a vast complex of tourist-related construction is underway, overlooking the recently completed Marina Herzliyya, which has also become a focus for high-tech industries.

NETANYA

Netanya is known as the 'diamond city', though for the most part this is an unexceptional, industrial place. However, the western strip of the city, with attractive clifftop gardens overlooking the azure Mediterranean, redeems Netanya's otherwise ordinary character. The city has a lot of budget-priced accommodation and is a popular package tour destination. With Jerusalem and the Galilee both less than 100km away and Tel Aviv near by to the south, and with good road, bus and even rail links, Netanya is strategically located for visitors who want just one base from which to see the whole of Israel while at the same time being close to those sandy white beaches.

WEST BANK (SAMARIA)

Since the start of the Palestinian uprising in 1987 most parts of the West Bank have been off limits for tourists. The granting of Palestinian autonomy to the largest cities has not stabilised the situation. However, should peace prevail, the potential for tourism in the northern part of the West Bank, known by the Israelis as Samaria (Shomeron), is enormous. The road northwards from Jerusalem passes through the affluent Palestinian town of Ramallah and on past beautiful biblical terrain dominated by terraced hills with olive groves and vineyards. Nablus (Shekhem), the largest city in Samaria, contains the tomb of Joseph and is home to a small community of Samaritans, who have maintained their pure Mosaic traditions for over 2,000 years. Further north is Sebaste, where the remains of King Ahab's palace and other ruins bear witness that this was once an important regional capital.

74B4
Restaurants and cafés (£–£££)
947 (from Jerusalem); 605 (from Tel Aviv)
Kikar Ha'atzmaut
☎ (09) 882 7286

75C3

Independence Square in Netanya is a focal point for visitors; in July and August a variety of open-air entertainments take place here

Eilat & the South

Though comprising nearly two-thirds of Israel's land mass, less than 10 per cent of the population lives here. This arid, compellingly attractive region is dominated by dramatic desert landscapes similar in terrain to the American West in Arizona. The Negev, however, also has unique crater formations and fascinating archaeological remains from previous civilisations – biblical, Nabatean and Byzantine. The Syria-Africa Rift Valley to the east rises southwards from the Dead Sea (▶ 19), the lowest point on earth, through the Arava Desert and on to Eilat, the Red Sea winter resort, which is Israel's second most popular tourist destination after Jerusalem. Large swathes of the south are out of bounds, taken over by the Israeli army as training grounds, and are clearly marked in English as 'firing zones'. Nevertheless, there are many nature reserves where the region's wildlife and natural assets can be seen, including the geological wonders of the Ramon Crater, the wildlife at Hay Bar and the fortress hideout at Masada.

> '*King Solomon built a navy in Ezion Geber, which is beside Eilat, on the shore of the Red Sea.*'

THE BIBLE, I Kings 9.26

———————●———————

King Solomon's Pillars, Timna National Park

Eilat

Eilat, Israel's southernmost town, sits on the northern tip of the Red Sea. The town itself is an unexceptional cluster of modern hotels set in an extremely attractive location. The surrounding desert mountains turn subtle hues of purple and red as the day progresses, in contrast to the sea's shades of silver and blue, making the Red Sea resemble a tranquil lake. Eilat also boasts abundant winter sunshine, with average January highs of 21°C (summer averages, however, soar to over 40°C). The town's most treasured asset is the Red Sea's extraordinary marine life with tropical fish of all shapes, sizes and colours and remarkable coral formations. Nature lovers can also view the millions of birds that migrate between Africa and Europe via Eilat each spring and autumn. The resort also makes a strategically located base for visiting Egypt's Sinai peninsula as well as the 'rose-red city' of Petra in Jordan.

Eilat flourished during biblical times when it stood to the east, where 'Aqaba is today. King Solomon expanded the city westwards when he established the port of Ezion Geber. The Israeli army conquered Eilat during the War of Independence but for several decades the town remained an isolated desert outpost. Massive hotel construction has characterised the past few decades, creating nearly 10,000 hotel rooms. The town is a favourite winter resort for

Palm-fringed North Beach is the perfect place for a swim

Europeans while the Israelis come here on holiday all year round. The port, Israel's outlet to the Far East, has developed rapidly on the back of burgeoning trade with Japan and Korea.

BIRDWATCHING CENTRE ✪

Eilat is an ornithologist's paradise as hundreds of millions of birds pass overhead each spring and autumn en route between their warm winter refuge in Africa and their breeding grounds in Europe. Eilat, between the desert and the sea, is a natural resting place. Among the multitude of birds there is a dazzling array of some 30 different species of raptor, including steppe, snake, lesser spotted and imperial eagles. A total of 400 different species altogether pass through, including pelicans, storks, osprey and marsh harriers. In addition there are several dozen species that are year-round residents in Eilat. The observation points, ringing station and hiking trails are northeast of the North Beach hotel district; the most rewarding time to visit is very early in the morning.

CORAL BEACH ✪

The Coral Beach is 5km south of the town centre, and being stonier than Eilat's main beaches, it is much less crowded. Moreover, there is some beautiful coral under the sea here, which is best viewed from the nearby **Coral Beach Nature Reserve**. Snorkelling and diving equipment can be hired from the hotel opposite. Several kilometres north of Coral Beach is the **Dolphin Reef**, a private beach where it is possible to swim with the dolphins. To the south of Coral Beach is the Coral World Underwater Observatory (➤ 18). Further south still is the Taba enclave on the border with Egypt. Taba itself is offically in Egypt but its hotel (with a casino) and beaches are open to all who simply show a passport.

🚩 82B1
✉ 61 Mercaz Tzenter
☎ (08) 637 4276
🕐 Birdwatching observation points daily from dawn–9:30AM
♿ Excellent
🎟 Free

Below: *swim with the dolphins at Dolphin Reef*

🚩 82B1

Coral Beach Nature Reserve
☎ (08) 637 6829
🕐 Daily 8–5
📅 15
♿ Excellent
🎟 Cheap

Dolphin Reef
☎ (08) 637 1846
🕐 Daily 9–5
📅 15
♿ Excellent
🎟 Moderate

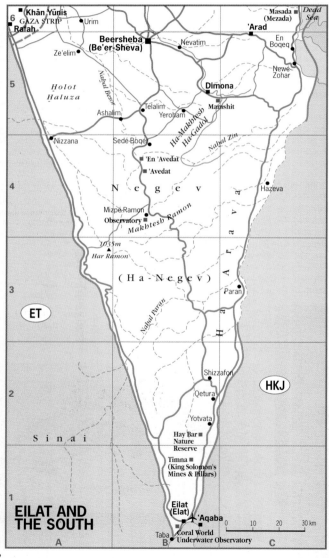

EILAT AND THE SOUTH

Map labels:

Khán Yúnis
GAZA STRIP
Rafah
Urim
Masada (Mezada)
Dead Sea
6
'Arad
Beersheba (Be'er-Sheva)
Nevatim
En Boqeq
Ze'elim
Newé Zohar
5
Holot Haluza
Nahal Besor
Dimona
Ashalim
Telalim
Yeroham
Mamshit
Nizzana
Sedé-Boqé
Ha-Makhtesh Ha-Gadol
Nahal Zin
'En 'Avedat
'Avedat
N e g e v
Hazeva
4
Mizpé-Ramon
Observatory
Makhtesh Ramon
Ha - 'Arava
1035m
Har Ramon
(Ha - Negev)
3
Paran
Nahal Paran
ET
Shizzafon
HKJ
2
Qetura
Yotvata
Sinai
Hay Bar Nature Reserve
Timna (King Solomon's Mines & Pillars)
Eilat (Elat)
'Aqaba
1
Taba
Coral World Underwater Observatory
0   10   20   30 km

A   B   C

Did you know ?

'Aqaba was the first city to be conquered by the Arab army led by Colonel Lawrence. Defeating the Ottoman Turks in 1917, Lawrence then used the town to receive arms shipments from Egypt.

What to See in the South

Below: *sun-shaded relics at 'En-Gedi*

'AQABA ★

Literally a stone's throw from Eilat, 'Aqaba was sealed off from its sister Red Sea resort until shortly after the Israel-Jordan peace accord in 1994. Jordan's only outlet to the sea is first and foremost a busy port. The tourist infra-structure in 'Aqaba is much smaller than in Eilat, but then the beaches are much quieter too. The site of the biblical Eilat, the name 'Aqaba was given to the city in the 14th century by the Mamelukes, who ruled over the region after defeating the Crusaders in the late 12th century. Excavations in the centre of town reveal remains from the past 2,000 years, while there is a Mameluke fortress at the southeastern end of town. There is a museum adjacent to the fortress exhibiting finds from the region.

✚ 82B1
☎ (08) 6336812
◉ Border crossing at Arava Checkpoint: Sun–Thu 6:30AM–10PM, Fri–Sat 8–8. Closed Yom Kippur and Id el Fitr
❓ Passport holders from the EU, US, Canada, Australia and New Zealand do not need visas to cross the border, but a border tax is payable on the Israeli side

'EN GEDI ★

'En Gedi, midway along the Dead Sea's western shore, is perhaps the most convenient place to take a 'float' in the salty water if you are not staying at one of the hotels in En Boqeq. There is even an artificial pebbly beach, which can get crowded on Fridays and Saturdays, and some rather pungent sulphur baths. Opposite 'En Gedi are two wadi nature reserves worth hiking in. **Nahal David**, the shorter of the two wadis, leads to a delightful cave covered by ferns beneath a waterfall, where, according to the Bible, David hid from Saul. **Nahal Arugot** also has attractive waterfalls and pools reached after a much longer trek.

✚ 28B3
🍴 Restaurant (£)
🚌 421, 444
♿ Excellent access to sea

Nahal Arugot and Nahal David Nature Reserves
☎ (07) 658 4285
◉ Apr–Oct, daily 8–4 (until 4PM Fri & Nov–Mar)
🎟 Cheap

Up Mount Tzefahot

Distance
6km

Time
4 hours including occasional stops

Start point
Eilat port
✚ 82B1

End point
Coral Beach
✚ 82B1

Lunch or tea
The Red Sea Divers Caravan
✉ Coral Beach
☎ (08) 637 3145/6

Relax on Coral Beach after your climb

This walk passes through spectacular desert terrain offering views of Eilat, the Red Sea and Sinai from the mountains and amid colourful rock formations. Due to its southerly latitude it is extremely hot in Eilat. Take plenty of water on this hike, at least two litres per person, and keep all parts of your body covered. Between March and November hike early in the morning or in the late afternoon, allowing time to return before dark.

Start the walk 4km south of Eilat (just past the port) by heading westwards along Nahal Shelomo (Solomon's Canyon).

The canyon is broad and surrounded by high hills. Mount Tzefahot is to the left. After 2km there is a group of buildings that once served as a quarantine station for imported animals. This complex marks the junction with Nahal Tzefahot, a canyon leading in from the left.

Take the path to the left along Nahal Tzefahot, which has green and white markings.

While walking along the bed of Nahal Tzefahot it is possible to appreciate the unusual type of rock found in the region. Granite, slate and other rocks are exposed, providing an attractive combination of red, black and dark-hued stone in addition to the colourful sandstone formed by erosion.

After 1km the canyon bed narrows and the path turns left out of the bed (still marked in green) and circumnavigates a steep drop above the Garinim Canyon. A path marked in black goes to the right, heading towards Sinai. Shortly after this junction the path turns to the right and ascends a narrow, steep canyon to Mount Tzefahot's summit.

The path passes just south of the summit but it is worth the final climb to savour the splendid view of the region from the 278m-high peak.

Return to the path and continue eastwards, exiting from the canyon opposite Coral Beach.

HA-MAKHTESH HA-GADOL (THE LARGE CRATER) ✪✪

This spectacular crater is located south of Dimona, near the town of Yeroham in the heart of the Negev Desert. Some ascribe the crater to volcanic activity and others to falling meteors. In any event there is a magnificent view from the observation point on the peak of Mount Evnon (656m); also worth seeing are the fossil forest (a geological site with stumps of fossilised trees) and the eucalyptus park where the strata of rock expose coloured sands. Ha-Makhtesh Ha-Katan (the Small Crater), much smaller and rounder in shape, is located 25km to the east, while the largest of the Negev's three craters, Makhtesh Ramon, is at Mizpé-Ramon, 55km to the south. This region was on the famous Nabatean spice route and near by are the Nabatean ruins of Mamshit. The site also has a camel ranch and a Nabatean restaurant.

➕ 82B5
🕐 Only worth visiting during daylight
🍴 No cafés in vicinity
🚌 No public transport – taxi from Dimona or Yerucham
♿ Excellent
🎟 Free

Above: antelope-like white oryx search for acacia leaves at the Hay Bar Nature Reserve

HAY BAR NATURE RESERVE ✪✪

Covering more than 3,000 hectares and located 50km north of Eilat, this unusual nature reserve seeks to reintroduce animals mentioned in the Bible as ubiquitous but which have become extinct over time. During the 90-minute minibus tour the visitor is likely to see wild asses, gazelles, ostriches and more. The 'predators centre' in the heart of the reserve houses indigenous raptors, reptiles and wild cats in zoo-like conditions. The ticket to Hay Bar includes entry to the Arava Visitors' Centre, which attractively exhibits and explains the history, geography, flora and fauna of the region.

➕ 82B2
☎ (08) 637 6018
🕐 Tours leave daily at 10, 11, 12, 1, 2 and 3 (the animals are more active during the earlier tours when it's cooler)
🍴 Café (£)
♿ Good
🎟 Moderate

85

➕ 28B3
📞 Hebron Municipality
(02) 996 1083
🍴 Restaurants (£)
🕐 Cave of Machpelah daily
4:30AM–9PM
🚌 160
♿ None
🎟 Free

HEBRON (HEVRON) ⊙

It was here, 37km south of Jerusalem, that Abraham, father of the Jewish and Arab peoples, purchased a plot of land as a family mausoleum. Since then more corpses have been buried in Hebron than Abraham bargained for. In 1929 Muslim extremists massacred the city's Jewish minority and since then both sides have initiated endless bloodshed, most recently when a Jewish extremist gunned down 30 Muslim worshippers in 1994. If peace prevailed, tourists would undoubtedly come to see the Cave of Machpelah, which contains the tombs of Abraham and his family, but with constant rioting and military closures only the adventurous are advised to visit at present. The situation has not improved since the western part of the town became a Palestinian autonomous zone in 1997. The eastern part, including the Cave of Machpelah, remains under Israeli jurisdiction.

➕ 82C6
📞 (08) 658 4207
🕐 Apr–Sep daily, 8–4; (until
3 Fri & eve of public
hols); Oct–Mar 8–3 (until
2 Fri & eve of public hols)
🍴 Café (£)
🚌 421, 444
♿ Few
🎟 Very expensive

The Northern Palace at Masada was Herod's private dwelling; surviving remains include a splendid bath house

MASADA ⊙⊙⊙

Built as a fortress and winter palace by Herod the Great in 40 BC, this mountain stronghold was seized by Jewish zealots after the uprising against Rome in AD 66. Over a thousand men, women and children held out against the Romans for seven years. But the Romans were determined to quash the rebellion and a legion of 15,000 Roman soldiers began building a mighty ramp to scale the 400m-high peak. When the zealots realised that all was lost they committed mass suicide rather than allow the Romans to capture them. If the story once inspired Israelis as one of heroism the behaviour of the zealots has in recent years increasingly become viewed as unnecessarily fanatical.

The fortress is reached either by cable-car or on foot via a zigzag track. The excavations reveal the luxury of Herod's palace, but most impressive of all is the view.

MIZPÉ-RAMON ●●

The largest of the three spectacular craters in the Negev Desert can be found at Mizpé-Ramon. The crater itself (Makhtesh Ramon) is best viewed from the visitors' centre to the east of the town. At the centre the visitor ascends through an exhibition describing this unusual geological phenomenon before reaching a panoramic window overlooking the crater itself. The crater is 300m deep, 8km wide and 40km long. Layer upon layer of colourful rocks are exposed and though it is not clear how the crater was formed, the strata of rocks in the crater itself reveal much about the geological evolution of the earth over many hundreds of million years. Fossilised plants and reptiles and dinosaur's footprints from 200 million years ago have been found here. Hiking trails are marked out and details are available at the visitors' centre. The town of Mizpé-Ramon itself, founded in 1954, is a somewhat depressing place, although it has an observatory belonging to Tel Aviv University and a research centre belonging to Ben Gurion University of the Negev.

✠ 82B4

☎ Visitors' centre (08) 658 8691

🕐 Visitors' centre: Sat–Thu 8–5, Fri 8–4

🍴 Restaurant (£)

🚌 60 (from Beersheba); 392 (from Beersheba and Eilat)

♿ Good

✋ Moderate

Left: Makhtesh Ramon provides many geological clues to the earth's evolution

Below: Bedouin still wander through the harsh desert landscape

From Eilat to Mizpé-Ramon

Distance
139km

Time
3–8 hours depending on stops

Start point
Eilat
✠ 82B1

End point
Mizpé-Ramon
✠ 82B4

Lunch
Hamiflat Haharon
Restaurant (£)
✉ Petrol station, Mizpé-
Ramon
☎ (07) 658 8158

Head north from Eilat on Highway 90. The border crossing into Jordan is 3km along the highway to the right. Another 10km further north tree lovers might want to see the world's most northerly domb palm tree, while another 2km further to the north is the spring of En Evrona. Both sites are marked from the highway with an orange sign.

The countryside in this part of the Arava, with hills on each side, is reminiscent of the American Wild West. Indeed many 'Westerns' have been shot on location here. Timna Park (➤ 90) is located on the right, 30km north of Eilat, while nearly 20km further along on the left is the Hay Bar Nature Reserve (➤ 85). Hay Bar is located on the salt desert by Kibbutz Yotvata, which is famous in Israel for its milk products. Try some in the café that belongs to the kibbutz, at the petrol station.

Continue along Highway 90 for another 10km to the Ketura Junction, turning left onto Highway 40.

After crossing the Grofit Plateau this road ascends some 500m into the hills. The highway then traverses a series of plateaux northwards before again ascending, for the last 10km, through the Ramon Crater (➤ 87) itself to Mizpé-Ramon, which is 1,000m above sea-level. On the road through the crater, there are information plaques every few hundred metres explaining the geological phenomena you can see.

The vast, arid expanse of Makhtesh Ramon

> ## Did you know ?
>
> *About a third of the Dead Sea Scrolls comprise the oldest known copy of the Old Testament, except for the Book of Esther. The levity of Esther's story, which features banquets, drunkenness and Esther's flirtation with the Persian king would not have suited Essene tastes. Many of the other scrolls describe the Essene way of life.*

These simple caves once held the secret of the Dead Sea Scrolls

QUMRAN ★★

It was in the caves above this Essene settlement, 20km south of Jericho, that a Bedouin shepherd boy found the first seven of the Dead Sea Scrolls in 1947. Well preserved in the dry desert climate, the papyrus and leather parchments were one of the most significant archaeological finds of the century. Some of the dozens of scrolls that have since been found are on display at the Israel Museum (➤ 20). The cave where the first scrolls were found can only be seen from a distance, but the Essene settlement from Roman times has been reconstructed. The Essenes were an austere monastic sect who lived around the time of Christ. They have captured the imagination because of speculation that they greatly influenced the philosophy and teaching of Christ himself. The Essenes were most unusual in their interpretation of Judaism, particularly in practising rigid asceticism and even celibacy.

+ 28B4
☎ (02) 994 2235
🕐 Apr–Sep, Sat–Thu 8–4:30, Fri 8–4; Oct–Mar, Sat–Thu, 8–4, Fri 8–3:30
🍴 Restaurant (£)
🚍 444 (Jerusalem–Eilat); 421 (Tel Aviv via Jerusalem)
♿ Excellent
👆 Moderate

SEDÉ-BOQÉR ★

Kibbutz Sedé-Boqér became famous when Israel's first Prime Minister, David Ben-Gurion, retired to this desert settlement 50km south of Beersheva. He lived here with his wife Paula from his retirement in 1953 until his death in 1973, except for the his second term in office (1955–63). The couple's grave, which lies south of the kibbutz, has become a place of pilgrimage for Israelis. From the graves there is a spectacular view of the Wilderness of Zin, where a popular hiking trail leads to the spring and pools of En Avdat. Sedé-Boqér now houses the Ben-Gurion Archives, which document the man's life and times.

+ 82B4
☎ (08) 656 0111
🚍 60 (from Beersheba); 392 (Beersheba–Eilat)
♿ Good

🕂 82A2

Details of border crossings:

Taba
☎ (08) 637 2104
🕔 Open 24 hours except for
Yom Kippur and Id el
Adkha

Nizzana
☎ (08) 655 5867
🕔 Daily 8–4

Rafah (Gaza Strip)
☎ (08) 673 4205
🕔 Daily 8:30–5

Above: *Sinai's Bedouin
tribesmen on the move*

🕂 82B1
☎ (08) 635 6215
🕔 Daily from 7:30–5 (until
6:30 in summer)
🍴 Café (£)
🚌 No public transport
♿ Good
 Moderate

SINAI ✪✪✪

Although Sinai is Egyptian territory, it is a popular excursion destination for visitors to Eilat. Sinai was held by Israel until 1982 after being captured in 1967 but the peninsula was returned to Egypt within the framework of the Israel-Egypt peace accord.

The Sinai is more rugged and spectacular than the Negev and everything is on a grander scale. The region's Mediterranean coast is less developed and less interesting than its Red Sea coast, where the marine life is even more fascinating than in Eilat. Moreover, it is possible to enter the Red Sea coast of Sinai at **Taba**, just south of Eilat, on a special two-week visa obtained at the border crossing. Those entering at **Nizzana** or **Rafah** or wanting to visit elsewhere in Egypt must obtain a visa from the Egyptian consulates in Eilat or Tel Aviv. Nuweiba is the settlement closest to Eilat, while Dahab and Sharm-el-Sheikh (where the best diving is) also have good hotels. A popular destination is St Catherine's Monastery, perched atop a mountain that many believe is the Mount Sinai from which Moses received the Ten Commandments.

TIMNA ✪

Timna National Park, situated 32km north of Eilat, contains the site of King Solomon's mines. Archaeologists estimate that copper mining began here 4,000 years ago, reaching its zenith a thousand years later under King Solomon. However, mining finally ceased in the 1970s because it was no longer profitable. A drive around the park takes in the impressive 50m-high King Solomon's Pillars and other rare rock formations, as well as an artifical lake.

Where To...

Above: *crocheted skull caps*
Right: *Palestinian vendor, Jerusalem*

Jerusalem

Prices
Approximate prices for a three-course meal for one person, with a glass of wine:

£ = under NIS75
££ = NIS75–250
£££ = over NIS250

Cheap Snacks
It is possible to eat very cheaply in Israel. Countless cafés in city centres ply inexpensive snacks such as falafel and *schwarma* (meat on a spit) served in pitta bread. Other popular snacks include *burekas* (cheese, potatoes or mushrooms in a crusty dough) and more universally known items like pizza, hot dogs and hamburgers.

Abu Shukri (£)
Located on the Via Dolorosa this Old City institution serves the best houmous and *ful* (beans) to be mopped up with pitta bread.
✉ 67 Ha-Gai Street
☎ (02) 627 1538 ⏰ Daily 8–5

Arcadia (£££)
Don't be fooled by the shabby alleyway leading to this restaurant – this is one of the city's finest eateries, set in beautiful surroundings. The best dishes on the menu are the goose liver, beef and grouper fish.
✉ 10 Agrippas Street
☎ (02) 624 9138 ⏰ Lunch, dinner. Closed Fri lunch

Armenian Tavern (£)
The best place to try out authentic Armenian food in a converted underground cistern near the Jaffa Gate. The owner enjoys explaining about the food and his country's history.
✉ 79 Armenian Patriarchate Road ☎ (02) 627 3854
⏰ Lunch, dinner. Closed Mon

Azzahra (££)
Located in East Jerusalem's commercial district, this attractive restaurant specializes in Arab cuisine. Try the *mezze* salads followed by stuffed lamb.
✉ 13 Azzahra Street
☎ (02) 628 2447 ⏰ Lunch, dinner

Café Atara (£)
Founded 68 years ago, Jerusalem's most famous café serves a range of lunch snacks, including an excellent onion soup. Café Atara has recently relocated to the Rehavya neighbourhood.
✉ 29 Azza Street ☎ (02) 561

8333 ⏰ Lunch, dinner. Closed Fri dinner, Sat lunch

Cardo Culinarium (££)
Diners are compelled to wear laurel wreaths and togas in a restaurant that was actually built by the Romans.
✉ The Cardo, Jewish Quarter, Old City ☎ (02) 626 4155
⏰ Lunch, dinner. Closed Fri dinner, Sat lunch

Cow on the Roof (£££)
Located in the basement, not on the roof, this prestigious French-style restaurant specialises in beef and lamb dishes.
✉ Sheraton Plaza Hotel, 47 King George Street ☎ (02) 629 8666 ⏰ Dinner. Closed Fri, Sat

Darna (£££)
A small corner of Morocco in Jerusalem. Enjoy north African food as part of an elegant ethnic experience using authentic implements and ceremonial service.
✉ 3 Horkenos Street ☎ (02) 624 5406 ⏰ Lunch, dinner. Closed Fri, Sat

Eucalyptus (£)
The owner is especially talented with herbs and spices, and attractively presents the traditional food of the land of Israel. Try the sorrel soup.
✉ 4 Safra Square ☎ (02) 624 4331 ⏰ Lunch, dinner. Closed Fri dinner, Sat lunch

Fink's (££)
Jerusalem's most famous bar is best known for its food rather than drink. Goulash soup is the dish to order, especially in winter.
✉ 13 King George Street
☎ (02) 623 4523 ⏰ Dinner. Closed Fri, Sat lunch

Hashipudia (£)

An excellent value steak house near Mahane Yehuda market. The name of the restaurant means 'the skewer', which is the speciality of the house.

✉ 6 Hashikma Street ☎ (02) 625 4036 🕐 Lunch, dinner. Closed Fri dinner, Sat lunch

Ima (£)

Pleasant Middle Eastern restaurant near the bus station. Try the *kubbe* soup and Jerusalem mixed grill or the delicious stuffed vegetables.

✉ 189 Agrippas Street ☎ (02) 624 6860 🕐 Lunch, dinner. Closed Fri dinner, Sat lunch

Katy's (£££)

Just off Jaffa Road in Nahalat Shiva, this restaurant serves classic French-style cooking with a North African influence in the sauces. Very intimate and elegant atmosphere.

✉ 2 Hasoreg Street ☎ (02) 623 1793 🕐 Lunch, dinner

Mishkenot Sha'ananim (£££)

Delightfully located in Yemin Moshe by the windmill with an inspiring view of the Old City, this restaurant is one of Jerusalem's best; it offers French cuisine with a Moroccan influence.

✉ Yemin Moshe ☎ (02) 625 1042 🕐 Lunch, dinner

Murduch (£)

Kurdish-style variations on all the other steak houses in the Mahane Yehuda area. Very popular and very good value so expect to queue.

✉ 70 Agrippas Street ☎ (02) 624 5169 🕐 Sun-Thu 8–5, Fri 8–3.30. Closed Sat

Ocean (£££)

This very expensive Italian-style fish restaurant is located in an attractive renovated building set in the heart of the Nahalat Shiva neighbourhood.

✉ 7 Rivlin Street ☎ (02) 624 7501 🕐 Lunch, dinner

Patio (££)

Fashionable lunchtime restaurant in the American Colony Hotel. Meals are served on the hotel's patio, hence the name.

✉ 1 Shekhem Street ☎ (02) 627 9777 🕐 Breakfast, lunch, dinner

Philadelphia East (££)

The best known of the Arab restaurants in East Jerusalem's commercial district. Excellent salads and meat served amid lavish Arabesque decor.

✉ 9 Azzahra Street ☎ (02) 628 9770 🕐 Lunch, dinner

La Regence (£££)

Situated Jerusalem's prestigious King David Hotel (► 102), La Regence is considered one of the best kosher restaurants in the world. The menu features the eclectic creations of young chef Rafi Cohen.

✉ 23 King David Street ☎ (02) 620 8888 🕐 Lunch, dinner

Rungsit (£££)

Named after a town in Thailand, this stylishly furnished restaurant (opposite the Laromme Jerusalem Hotel) offers kosher Thai/Japanese food. Try the duck.

✉ 2 Jabotinsky Street ☎ (02) 561 1757 🕐 Lunch, dinner. Closed Fri dinner, Sat lunch

Paying

Many restaurants do not include service in the bill. A typical Israeli gratuity is 10 per cent, but service can be very poor and you may not feel like tipping. Most restaurants accept foreign credit cards but check first. By law a restaurant must provide you with an itemised bill.

Water

Israeli water is perfectly drinkable although environmentalists are increasingly warning that levels of pollution are too high. Bottled mineral water is widely available both in restaurants and from street kiosks, and from March to October it is advisable to drink large quantities of water when sightseeing. The number of tourists hospitalised for dehydration every year is remarkably high.

Sami (£)

Popular eatery near Mahane Yehuda with all the local steakhouse specialities, including Jerusalem mixed grill, *shishlik*, kebab, heart and various other parts of the anatomy. Often has standing room only.

✉ 80 Agrippas Street ☎ (02) 625 0985 🕐 Lunch, dinner. Closed Fri dinner, Sat lunch

Sakura (££)

A kosher sushi restaurant serving a variety of fish located in an attractive courtyard off bustling Jaffa Street. Also has excellent tea-flavoured ice cream.

✉ Finegold Court by 31 Jaffa Street ☎ 🕐 Lunch, dinner. Closed Fri dinner, Sat lunch

Sergio's Friends (££)

An alien but excellent Italian restaurant in the heart of Mahane Yehuda's Middle Eastern eateries. More spacious (and expensive) than most of its neighbours.

✉ 34 Agrippas Street ☎ (02) 625 5665 🕐 Lunch, dinner. Closed Fri dinner, Sat lunch

Shalom (£)

For a few dollars it is possible to get your fill of falafel from first thing in the morning until last thing at night. Not much larger than a kiosk.

✉ 38 Bezalel Street ☎ (02) 623 1436 🕐 Lunch, dinner. Closed Fri dinner, Sat lunch

Shemesh (££)

Middle Eastern food in a busy spot in central Jerusalem. Try a salad starter followed by a hearty grill or kebab.

✉ Ben Yehuda Street ☎ (02) 625 3232 🕐 Lunch, dinner. Closed Fri dinner, Sat lunch

Sima (£)

Best known of the eateries in Agrippas Street, this is no place to linger over your meal. Excellent value but the staff take pride in their speed of service and the haste with which customers are expected to bolt down their food.

✉ 82 Agrippas Street ☎ (02) 623 3002 🕐 Lunch, dinner. Closed Fri dinner, Sat lunch

Spaghettim (££)

As well as the good food, including all the Italian favourites, this restaurant has the added bonus of being located in a beautiful house and courtyard in the town centre.

✉ 8 Rabbi Akiva Street ☎ (02) 623 5547 🕐 Lunch, dinner

Taverna (£££)

Extremely attractive decor, both interior and exterior, and stunning view of the Judean Desert make this an enchanting restaurant. The food is not bad either.

✉ 2 Naomi Street, Abu Tor ☎ (02) 671 9796 🕐 Lunch, dinner. Closed Sun

Le Tsriff (££)

This veteran Jerusalem restaurant is set in a wooden building in the heart of the city's restaurant district.

✉ 5 Horkenos Street ☎ (02) 624 2478 🕐 Lunch, dinner. Closed Yom Kippur

Valentino's (££)

This pleasant Italian restaurant in the Hyatt Regency hotel on Mount Scopus offers all the Italian staples at reasonable prices.

✉ Lehi Street, French Hill ☎ (02) 629 8666 🕐 Lunch, dinner

Galilee & the North

'Akko

Hamudi Restaurant (£)
Small eatery in Old 'Akko serving houmous and *ful* as well as skewered meats and all the basic Middle Eastern staples. Excellent value and very cheap.

✉ 35 Ha'arbaa Street ☎ (04) 991 7606 🕙 Breakfast, lunch, early dinner (closes 8PM). Closed Fri dinner

The Western Beach (££)
Situated near the police station and the sea wall, this is the pick of the fish restaurants in 'Akko. Excellent salads are served here too.

✉ 4 Hahagana Street ☎ (04) 991 9666 🕙 Lunch, dinner

Haifa

Falafel-Michel (£)
This simple, clean and very cheap eatery offers falafel, houmous and other Middle Eastern basics. Falafel-Michel is located in Haifa's somewhat dilapidated Wadi Nisnas Arab quarter just south of the port area.

✉ 21 Hawadi Street, Wadi Nisnas ☎ (04) 851 4959 🕙 Lunch, dinner

Grill-Fish (££)
Despite the mundane-sounding name, this restaurant serves an excellent range of fish with tasty accompanying salads. Situated in Bat Galim, in the south of the city, near the central bus and train stations.

✉ 27 Margolin Street ☎ (04) 852 6779 🕙 Lunch, dinner. Closed Fri dinner, Sat lunch

Nof Chinese Restaurant (££)
This kosher Chinese restaurant, located in the Nof Hotel, offers good food along with a spectacular and romantic view of Haifa Bay.

✉ 101 Hanassi Boulevard ☎ (04) 835 4311 🕙 Lunch, dinner

The Old Man and The Sea (£££)
Excellent fish cuisine served in a restaurant with unusual decor. Located in a city centre mall.

✉ 6 Ben Gurion Boulevard ☎ (04) 850 7777 🕙 Lunch, dinner

Shawarma Emile (£)
Located in the port in downtown Haifa this restaurant specialises in meat cut from the spit as well as a wide range of vegetables and pickled relishes to accompany it with chips or in pitta.

✉ 33 Allenby Street ☎ (04) 851 7096 🕙 Lunch, dinner

Taiwan (££)
This restaurant can be found opposite the Baha'i Shrine and is situated in an attractive wooden house in beautiful gardens. The food is Chinese/Thai and a relatively cheap business lunch is good value for tourists visiting the Baha'i gardens.

✉ 59 Ben Gurion Boulevard ☎ (04) 853 2082 🕙 Lunch, dinner

Voilà (££)
Franco-Swiss restaurant with country-style decor in a garden-house in midtown Hadar's pedestrian mall. Good choice of salads, meats and seafood.

✉ 21 Nordau Street, Hadar ☎ (04) 866 4529 🕙 Lunch, dinner

Soft Drinks
All the usual carbonated drinks are available in Israel – Coke, Pepsi, 7 Up and so on. Fruit juices are widely available but in cheaper restaurants tend not to be pure, so be sure to specify if you want 100 per cent juice. Best of all are the streetside kiosks crammed full of fruit waiting to be freshly squeezed for thirsty passers-by. It is amazing how much better juice tastes and quenches a thirst when it has just been squeezed.

Beer

Beer lovers will find little to satisfy them in Israel. Beer comes in two varieties – light (lager) and dark (bitter). Local brews are Goldstar (bitter) and Maccabi (lager); also available brewed under license are Tuborg and Heineken. Beer is usually drunk from the bottle though draught is available in bars and some restaurants. The little beer that is available is poorly maintained and in the heat of the summer is usually flat.

Yankale Restaurant (£)

Romanian cuisine served in the heart of midtown Hadar. Plain, straightforward, unpretentious food served by polite staff.

⊠ 26 Hameginim Boulevard ☎ (04) 851 1363 ⏰ Breakfast, lunch

Majdel Shams
Hashalom (£)

This restaurant – located in the foothills of Mount Hermon and one of Israel's highest – serves excellent Middle Eastern food.

⊠ Northern entrance to Majdel Shams ☎ (04) 698 3140 ⏰ Breakfast, lunch, dinner

Nazareth
Diana (££)

Good-quality Middle Eastern fare featuring excellent salads, kebabs and lamb chops. Located on the main street near the Basilica of the Annunciation.

⊠ 51 Paul the Sixth Road ☎ (04) 657 2919 ⏰ Breakfast, lunch, dinner

El Sheikh (£)

Very cheap but good-quality Middle Eastern food, including great houmous. The restaurant is ocated in an industrial area just outside the town centre.

⊠ Afifi Building, Iksal Street ☎ (04) 656 7664 ⏰ Breakfast, lunch

Rosh-Pinna
HaKfar (££)

HaKfar offers Latin American cuisine in the centre of this picturesque village.

⊠ The Old Road ☎ (04) 693 8026 ⏰ Lunch, dinner

Rafa's House (££)

This South American restaurant is situated in a renovated stone building with interesting arches and an outdoor terrace. The menu features steaks, casserole-type dishes and vegetarian options.

⊠ Upper Street, Old Rosh-Pinna ☎ (04) 693 6192 ⏰ Lunch, dinner

Safed
Shipudei Zefat (£)

Standard Middle Eastern food in the centre of town with a wonderful view of the surrounding mountains.

⊠ 49 Jerusalem Street ☎ (04) 692 1979 ⏰ Lunch, dinner. Closed Fri dinner, Sat lunch

Tiberias
Galei Gil (££)

This veteran fish restaurant overlooks the lake. A range of well-seasoned fish is offered, with St Peter's fish (*tilapia*) being the local speciality.

⊠ The Old Promenade ☎ (04) 672 0699 ⏰ Lunch, dinner

Guy (£)

Good-value eatery on the road south to Beit She'an which serves straight-forward Middle Eastern fare in a comfortable environment.

⊠ Hagalil Street ☎ (04) 672 1973 ⏰ Lunch, dinner. Closed Fri dinner, Sat lunch

The Pagoda (££)

One of Israel's best known Chinese restaurants is located at the northern entrance to Tiberias overlooking the lake. Good value Thai/Chinese cuisine.

⊠ Opposite Lido Beach ☎ (04) 672 5513 ⏰ Lunch, dinner

Tel Aviv-Jaffa

Bellini (££)

This is a charming Italian restaurant with wood-burning fireplaces and attractive kitchens which are open to the view of the diners. Good, tasty food served in a pleasant atmosphere.

✉ **6 Yechiely Street, Suzanne Dallal Centre** ☎ **(03) 517 8486** 🕐 **Lunch, dinner**

Cactus (££)

An excellent haunt for those who crave spicy Mexican food. Situated near the US embassy, the house specialities at Cactus include black bean purée and, inevitably, the ever popular chilli con carne.

✉ **66 HaYarkon Street** ☎ **(03) 510 5969** 🕐 **Lunch, dinner**

David's Ful (£)

This kosher establishment in the Yemenite quarter specialises in Egyptian food and in particular *ful* dishes. Inexpensive, savoury cooking and some tables even look into the kitchen.

✉ **22 Peduim Street** ☎ **(03) 516 0693** 🕐 **Lunch, dinner. Closed Fri dinner, Sat lunch**

Dr Shakshuka (£)

Next to Jaffa's flea market this simple restaurant offers good Libyan cuisine. A 'sampling menu' is a very good value way of tasting everything.

✉ **3 Bet Eshel Street, Jaffa** ☎ **(03) 682 2842** 🕐 **Lunch, dinner. Closed Fri dinner, Sat lunch**

Elimelech (££)

Excellent place for those who pine for traditional Eastern European kosher food. Located in a small restaurant south of the business district.

✉ **35 Wolfson Street** ☎ **(03) 681 3459** 🕐 **Lunch, dinner**

Espresso Bar

A rich choice of coffees available in the elegant Rothschild Bouldevard.

✉ **48 Rothschild Boulevard** ☎ **(03) 510 8919**

Jonathan Roshfeld (£££)

The city's most fashionable, and most expensive, restaurant serving the finest French food and wine in simple but elegant surroundings.

✉ **23 King Saul Boulevard** ☎ **(03) 695 2448** 🕐 **Dinner**

Mifgash Ha'Balkan (££)

This Jaffa restaurant serves Balkan delicacies such as cheese-stuffed eggplants and leek patties.

✉ **43 Jerusalem Street, Jaffa** ☎ **(03) 683 0719** 🕐 **Lunch, dinner. Closed Sun**

Moul Yam (£££)

This is one of Tel Aviv's finest restaurants, offering succulent (unkosher) seafoods such as lobster and oysters as well as fish; all are pulled live, according to customer choice, out of the aquarium.

✉ **Tel Aviv Port** ☎ **(03) 546 9920** 🕐 **Lunch, dinner**

New York New York (££)

As the name suggests, this restaurant offers New York-style wholesome food with deli sandwiches, steaks and help-yourself salads. There is also a branch in Herzliyya.

✉ **30 Ibn Gbriol Street** ☎ **(03) 695 1541** 🕐 **Lunch, dinner**

Wine

Even in Israel's finest restaurants wine is not viewed as compulsory. Although wine is an integral part of Jewish ritual, drinking more than a glass or two is seen as drunken and decadent. Table wines tend to be expensive and poor quality, but try such labels as Golan, Ben Ami, Dalton and Carmel's Rothschild Series, which are good if rather pricey.

Coffee

It is customary in Middle Eastern restaurants to drink Turkish coffee (which is often on the house) after the meal. A local variation of Turkish coffee known affectionately as *botz* (meaning mud), is sometimes served. These coffees come with sugar already in them. *Cafe Hafuch*, a local variation of capuccino, is very popular, while regular Western-style coffee is known as *nes*.

Pasta Mia (££)

This vegetarian Italian restaurant makes its own tasty pasta and a range of delicious original sauces. The menu also features a choice of salads and cakes.

✉ **10 Wilson Street** ☎ **(03) 561 0189** ⏰ **Lunch. Closed evenings and Sat**

Patisserie (£)

More of a café than a restaurant, as the name implies, this establishment serves good-value snacks such as sandwiches and salads as well as enticing cakes and excellent coffee.

✉ **16 Masarik (near Rabin Square)** ☎ **(03) 524 2962** ⏰ **Lunch, dinner**

Rachmo Hagadol (£)

Excellent, clean and astonishingly cheap place for falafel, houmous, *ful* etc. Not far from the old Central Bus Station.

✉ **98 Petah Tikvah Street** ☎ **(03) 562 1022** ⏰ **Lunch, dinner**

Shmulik Cohen (££)

From *gefilte* fish to chicken soup and *kishkes*, this great-value restaurant offers a good choice of traditional Yiddish food. The proprietor's father founded the restaurant in 1920 when Tel Aviv was little more than a village.

✉ **146 Herzl Street** ☎ **(03) 681 0222** ⏰ **Lunch, dinner. Closed Fri dinner and Sat**

Stamboul (££)

Small and clean, this Turkish restaurant is in the very trendy Florentin neighbourhood near Jaffa. Excellent *mezze* salads and grilled meats.

✉ **16 Uriel Acosta Street,** Florentin ☎ **(03) 681 2588** ⏰ **Lunch, dinner**

Taboon (£££)

Taboon is Arabic for oven, and this restaurant, delightfully situated by Jaffa port, specialises in tasty baked fish.

✉ **Jaffa Port** ☎ **(03) 681 6011** ⏰ **Lunch, dinner**

Taj Mahal (£££)

Not quite *the* Taj Mahal but nevertheless located in a very impressive old building in Jaffa overlooking the sea. Authentic Indian cuisine with delicious chicken dishes.

✉ **12 Kedumim Square, Old Jaffa** ☎ **(03) 682 1002** ⏰ **Lunch, dinner**

Tznobar (££)

This restaurant, the name means pine kernel, offers an unusual blend of Eastern and Western cooking.

✉ **293 Dizengoff Street** ☎ **(03) 544 3427** ⏰ **Lunch, dinner**

Yakimono (££)

Delightful Japanese restaurant and sushi bar located in old Tel Aviv port. Pleasant fare at reasonable prices.

✉ **5 Yordey Hasira Street** ☎ **(03) 544 3864** ⏰ **Lunch, dinner**

Zion (££)

One of the best known and longest established restaurants in the Yemenite quarter, the Zion offers a choice of eating options. There is the an inexpensive eatery downstairs and the more expensive restaurant, called 'The Exclusive', upstairs.

✉ **28 Peduim Street** ☎ **(03) 517 8714** ⏰ **Daily 11AM–1AM. Closed Fri dinner, Sat lunch.**

Central Region

Ashkelon

Hakhan (£)

This restaurant is in an old Arab *khan* (inn) that has been pleasantly renovated. Middle Eastern food and excellent fish dishes complement the decor.

✉ 1 Kikar Ha'atamaut ☎ (08) 672 2220 🕐 Lunch, dinner. Closed Fri lunch

Bat Yam

Shipudei Tzipora (£)

This restaurant in the relatively cheap resort of Bat Yam, south of Jaffa, offers good value, standard Middle Eastern fare such as *mezze* salads and skewered meat.

✉ 5 Bar Shaul Street ☎ (03) 659 7925 🕐 Lunch, dinner

Herzliyya

Bella Venezia (££)

Italian restaurant located in Herzliyya's high-tech industrial park just off the Tel Aviv–Haifa highway. All the usual pasta favourites and good soups too.

✉ 21 Yad Harutzim Street ☎ (09) 957 6126 🕐 Lunch, dinner

Tandoori (££)

Also in the high-tech industrial zone, this restaurant specialises in tandoori dishes. Especially good are the chicken and lamb tandooris.

✉ 5 Maskit Street ☎ (09) 954 6702 🕐 Lunch, dinner

White House (££)

American-style restaurant serving excellent steaks, delicious French fries and a good choice of self-service salads.

✉ Hagalim Boulevard, corner of Maskit Street ☎ (09) 958 0402 🕐 Lunch, dinner

Netanya

El Gaucho (££)

Part of a nationwide chain of Argentinian restaurants that serves up massive, well-seasoned steaks. Located in the Carmel Hotel, there is a great view of the sea over the cliffs.

✉ Jabotinsky Street ☎ (09) 884 1264 🕐 Lunch, dinner. Closed Fri dinner, Sat lunch

Lucullus (££)

Deceptively situated in a shabby-looking commercial centre, this restaurant offers classic French cuisine.

✉ 2 Jabotinsky Street ☎ (09) 861 9502 🕐 Lunch, dinner

Samovar (££)

One of a new crop of Russian restaurants opened by newcomers from the former Soviet Union. Russian décor and vodka add to the ethnic experience.

✉ 1 Sha'ar Haemek Street ☎ (09) 833 3397 🕐 Lunch, dinner

Ramla

Yellow Chinese (££)

This is considered the country's finest Chinese restaurant, despite its location in a petrol station on the bypass road of one of Israel's poorest towns.

✉ Paz Station, Ramla ring road ☎ (08) 923 3149 🕐 Lunch, dinner

Rishon le-Ziyyon

Rothschilds (£££)

Up-market name and address for a restaurant that offers up-market food and even has its own wine room – unusual in Israel.

✉ 83 Rothschild Boulevard ☎ (03) 964 1350 🕐 Lunch, dinner

Tea

Those who enjoy Western-style tea will have a difficult time in Israel where weak tea-bags are placed into water. It's better to try many of the herbal teas. Locals sip tea with mint or cloves or other herbs and add large heaps of sugar. Tea is rarely drunk with milk.

Eilat & the South

Parve

Parve is the Hebrew word for something that, within the context of kosher dietary laws, can be eaten with either meat or milk. It includes fruit and vegetables but usually refers to a substitute milk, ice-cream or other dairy product served after meat. In practice *parve* is entirely artificial and is therefore best avoided for reasons of both taste and health.

'Arad

Mister Shai (££)
Excellent Chinese restaurant in this pleasant desert town; the fantastic view of the Dead Sea region is an added bonus.
✉ **32 Hapalmach Street** ☎ **(08) 997 1956** 🕐 **Lunch, dinner. Closed Sun**

Beersheba

Ezra Zion (£)
Worth visting if you go to the Bedouin market. Great-value restaurant with excellent choice of skewered meats.
✉ **1 Shazar Street** ☎ **(08) 623 5813** 🕐 **Lunch, dinner**

Sami & Susu (££)
This restaurant is actually by the Bedouin market. Specialises in grilled meats and home-pickled fish but gets very crowded on market day.
✉ **179–80 New Market** ☎ **(08) 624 5819** 🕐 **Lunch, dinner. Closed Fri dinner and Sat**

Dead Sea

'En Gedi Guest House (£)
Good food, especially the meat and salads, but best of all the restaurant offers a fabulous view of the Dead Sea and surrounding mountains.
✉ **Kibbutz 'En Gedi** ☎ **(08) 659 4222** 🕐 **Breakfast, lunch and dinner**

Mifgash Zohar (£)
At the northern tip of the Dead Sea, this roadside establishment offers excellent meals for those en route between Jerusalem, the Dead Sea, Eilat and Jericho.
✉ **Almog Junction** ☎ **(02) 994 2423** 🕐 **Breakfast, lunch and dinner**

Petra (££)
Vegetarian and dairy food offered with a view of the Dead Sea. The restaurant is located in the En Boqeq commercial centre by the hotel complex.
✉ **En Boqeq Centre** ☎ **(08) 658 4477** 🕐 **Lunch, dinner**

Pundak 'En Gedi (£)
Another good restaurant located by a petrol station. Wholesome self-service canteen food at reasonable prices to satisfy the hunger generated by long car journeys through inspiring landscapes.
✉ **'En Gedi petrol station** ☎ **(08) 659 4761** 🕐 **Breakfast, lunch (closes daily 5PM)**

Eilat

Au Bistro (£££)
One of the town's classiest restaurants serving traditional French food at its best. Makes a change from the over-designed décor in Eilat's hotels.
✉ **3 Eilot Street** ☎ **(08) 637 4333** 🕐 **Dinner**

La Brasserie (£££)
Located in the attractive King Solomon's Palace Hotel, this restaurant, as the name implies, attempts to be a French-style brasserie and succeeds very well.
✉ **King Solomon Palace Hotel, North Beach** ☎ **(08) 636 3444** 🕐 **Dinner. Closed Fri**

Chao Phya (£££)
Like the Orchid Hotel to which this restaurant belongs, Chao Phya is a wooden Thai-style structure. The Thai food completes the ethnic experience.
✉ **Orchid Hotel, South Beach**

☎ (08) 636 0335 🕐 Lunch, dinner. Closed Fri dinner, Sat lunch

La Cuccina (££)
One of the best Italian restaurants in Eilat. Located on the seafront on the North Beach. Specialises in non-meat dishes.
✉ Royal Beach promenade, North Beach ☎ (08) 636 8932 🕐 Dinner. Closed Sat, Sun

El Gaucho (££)
Another branch of Israel's Argentinian restaurant chain. Serves up giant portions, so don't over-order.
✉ 2 Ha'arava Road ☎ (08) 633 1549 🕐 Lunch, dinner

The Last Refuge (£££)
Hidden away on a jetty by Coral Beach, the sound of the lapping waves all around whets the appetite at this excellent fish and seafood restaurant.
✉ Coral Beach ☎ (08) 637 2437 🕐 Lunch, dinner

Mamen Dagim (£)
A good-value fish restaurant with a pleasant location along the seafront. As with all Israeli fish dishes, what is lacking in substance is made up for in interesting seasoning.
✉ North Beach by the Radisson Moriah Plaza Hotel ☎ (08) 637 1958 🕐 Lunch, dinner

Meurav Eilat (£)
Standard Middle Eastern fare of salads and grilled meats on skewers for the budget-conscious. Opposite the central bus station.
✉ 127 HaTamarim Boulevard ☎ (08) 637 1215 🕐 Lunch, dinner

Palms (££)
Excellent value restaurant in the stylish Princess Hotel by the Egyptian border. Enjoy your fish on the veranda looking out to the Red Sea.
✉ Princess Hotel, near Taba ☎ (08) 636 5555 🕐 Dinner. Closed Fri

Regata (££)
Located in the Dan Eilat, which is considered one of the town's finest hotels, this restaurant specialises in fish and dairy dishes and enjoys a view of the beach and sea.
✉ Dan Eilat Hotel, North Beach ☎ (08) 636 2293 🕐 Lunch, dinner

Wang's Grill (££)
A Pacific Rim-style restaurant combining Far Eastern and US recipes as is the trend in California, and thereby creating one of the best kosher restaurants in Israel.
✉ Royal Beach Hotel, North Beach ☎ (08) 636 8888 🕐 Dinner. Closed Fri

Mizpé-Ramon
Hamiflat Haharon (£)
Good-value self-service restaurant offering a range of meat dishes. Filling stuff.
✉ In front of the visitors' center ☎ (08) 658 8158 🕐 Lunch, dinner

Yotvata
Yotvata Café (£)
Good cafeteria on the main Eilat/Arava highway. Worth sampling the rich dairy drinks (flavoured milks) for which the kibbutz is famed.
✉ Kibbutz Yotvata ☎ (08) 635 7449 🕐 Breakfast, lunch

Nabatean Nosh
The Dushara Restaurant at the Mamshit archaeological site near Dimona, where there are Nabatean and Byzantine remains, is the world's only Nabatean restaurant. The staff wear Nabatean outfits, the décor is reconstructed Nabatean and the food is a mixture of the grains, fruit, vegetables and meats that the Nabateans, Middle Eastern traders, ate.
☎ (08) 655 5596 🕐 Lunch, dinner

Jerusalem & Environs

Prices (in US dollars) for double room
£   = up to $90
££   = $90–$150
£££ = above $150
Price for double room usually includes breakfast.

Good Morning Jerusalem ☎ (02) 651 1270 gives information on all available B&Bs in the city. Double rooms cost no more than $60.

Booking

As the above prices indicate, it is very expensive simply to turn up. It is far cheaper, something between 20–33 per cent of these prices, to book a package deal overseas. All hotels happily accept credit cards and exempt those paying in foreign currency from 17 per cent VAT. There is no VAT in Eilat. Hotel rates are generally quoted in US dollars and include a 15 per cent service charge.

American Colony (£££)
Established in the 19th century, this is Jerusalem's oldest hotel. Still owned by its founding American Christian family, the hotel is preferred by the foreign press corps because of its 'neutral' location between West and East Jerusalem.
✉ Shekhem Street ☎ (02) 627 9777; fax: (02) 627 9779

Caesar Hotel (£)
Smack opposite the central bus station, this modern, unexceptional hotel is ideally located for itinerant tourists on a limited budget.
✉ 208 Jaffa Street ☎ (02) 500 5656; fax: (02) 538 2802

Hilton (£££)
Jerusalem's newest hotel is situated near the Jaffa Gate and is attractively designed and well appointed.
✉ 1 King David Street ☎ (02) 621 1111; fax: (02) 621 1000

Holiday Inn Crowne Plaza (££)
This landmark high-rise beacon at the city entrance is one of the city's most fashionable hotels.
✉ Givat Ram ☎ (02) 658 8888; fax: (02) 652 7097

Inbal (£££)
Modern, popular hotel (formerly the Laromme) overlooking the Old City, offering good value in its class.
✉ 3 Jasotinsky Street ☎ (02) 675 6666

Itzik (£)
Comfortable and clean with a fascinating location in the heart of the Mahane Yehuda market. Also near the Central Bus Station.

✉ 141 Jaffa Street ☎ (02) 624 3879; fax: (02) 623 3730

King David (£££)
Jerusalem's most prestigious hotel has an old-world ambience and attractive gardens overlooking the Old City. Once the rich and famous automatically stayed here but the hotel is now facing stiff competition from its younger rivals.
✉ 23 King David Street ☎ (02) 620 8888; fax: (02) 623 2303

Mitzpeh Ramat Rachel (££)
This attractive guest house in the well-tended grounds of the kibbutz on Jerusalem's southern city limit offers a spectacular view of the Judean Desert.
✉ Kibbutz Ramat Rachel ☎ (02) 670 2555; fax: (02) 673 3155

Notre Dame (££)
One of Jerusalem's most inspiring 19th-century buildings, this hospice offers luxurious accommodation as well as a great restaurant.
✉ Hatzankhanim Street, opposite the New Gate ☎ (02) 627 9111; fax: (02) 627 1995

Our Sisters of Zion (££)
Provence-style pension in rural 'En Kerem. Managed by nuns and set amid citrus groves and grape vines.
✉ Ha'akhayot Street, 'En Kerem ☎ (02) 641 5738; fax: (02) 643 7739

Ron (£)
In the heart of downtown Jerusalem, this hotel resembles a European pension.
✉ 44 Jaffa Street ☎ (02) 625 3471; fax: (02) 625 0707

Galilee & the North

'Akko
Palm Beach (££)
An ordinary hotel but for two things. It has its own private Mediterranean beach and is just 20 minutes' walk from ancient 'Akko.

✉ Sefat Hayam Street ☎ (04) 981 5815; fax: (04) 991 0434

Haifa
Dan Carmel (£££)
On the summit of Mount Carmel, this stylish hotel offers a breathtaking view of the Mediterranean below.

✉ 85-87 Harvasi Avenue ☎ (04) 830 3030; fax: (04) 838 7504

Dvir (£)
An ordinary hotel that offers an exceptional view of the bay from atop Mount Carmel at budget prices.

✉ 124 Yefe Nof ☎ (04) 838 9131; fax: (04) 838 1068

Tiberias
Aviv (£)
This simple, compact hotel is within easy walking distance of the sea and offers very good-value accommodation.

✉ 66 Hagalil ☎ (04) 672 0007; fax: (04) 672 3510

Howard Johnson Plaza
Pleasantly situated along the shore of the lake, this was the city's first luxury hotel.

✉ 1 Eliezer Kaplan Street ☎ (04) 679 2231; fax: (04) 679 2320

Upper Galilee
Amirim (£)
This co-operative village (*moshav*) is completely vegetarian. Situated in the Meron Mountains near Safed and surrounded by scenic views of the Sea of Galilee, it is devoted to tourism.

✉ Moshav Amirim, Merom Hagalil ☎ (04) 698 9232; fax: (04) 698 0772

Hagoshrim (££)
Kibbutz guest house in the lap of the Galilee countryside. Makes a convenient base to tour the Sea of Galilee and Golan Heights.

✉ Kibbutz Ayelet Hashahar, Upper Galilee ☎ (04) 681 6000; fax: (04) 681 6002

Kfar Blum (££)
Pleasant rural surroundings on this Upper Galilee kibbutz with the River Jordan flowing through the middle of the settlement.

✉ Kibbutz Kfar Blum, Upper Galilee ☎ (04) 683 6611; fax: 683 6600

Metulla
Arazim (£)
Comfortable, rustic pension-style hotel in the cool altitudes of Metulla on the Lebanese border. The name *Ha'arazim* appropriately means 'the cedars'.

✉ Harishonim Street ☎ (04) 699 7144; fax: (04) 699 7666

Safed
Howard Johnson Plaza Ruth Rimon Inn (£££)
The most characterful hotel in the Galilee, located in the heart of the artists' quarter and enjoying hillside views.

✉ Artists' Quarter ☎ (04) 692 0665; fax: (04) 692 0456

Ron (£)
Mid-range hotel with decent rooms and restaurant. Only 10 minutes' walk from the main sights.

✉ near Metzuda ☎ (04) 692 2590

Unique Accommodation
Like any other country Israel has a diverse cross-section of over 300 hotels, from the budget priced to the luxuriously exorbitant. But Israel has two types of unique accommodation. The kibbutz guest house offers the facilities of a comfortable country club style hotel as well as the chance to get acquainted with these unique socialist collectives. The Christian hospice, designed for pilgrims and owned by churches, nevertheless offers great comfort rather than sackcloth and ashes, usually with 19th-century European character.

Tel Aviv & the Central Region

When to Book

Hotels are most expensive during religious festivals such as Passover/Easter, the Jewish High Holy Days (Sep/Oct) and Christmas. July and August is also peak season. The best and cheapest time to visit, also from the weather point of view, is the late autumn, November. In Eilat however, prices are most expensive between November and March.

Ashkelon
Village (fomerly Dagon, £)
This small hotel is quiet, comfortable and affordable – and close to the sea.
✉ **2 Rehov Moshe Dorot**
☎ **(08) 673 6111; fax: (08) 673 0666**

Herzliyya
Dan Accadia (£££)
Owned by the Dan chain, like Jerusalem's King David, this is one of Israel's oldest hotels and is more elegant than its rather brash neighbours.
✉ **Derekh Hayam** ☎ **(09) 959 7070; fax: (09) 959 7090**

Netanya
Goldar (£)
Clean and comfortable and located by the city's central square, about three minutes' walk from the seafront.
✉ **1 Ussishkin Street**
☎ **(09) 833 8188; fax: (09) 862 0680**

Grand Yahalom (£)
Small establishment located in the heart of Netanya's hotel district, but still no more than five minutes away from the beach below.
✉ **15 Gad Machness Street**
☎ **(09) 862 4888; fax: (09) 862 4890**

Tel Aviv-Yafo
Adiv (£)
Situated several streets inland from the sea, this small but comfortable hotel has a good-value self-service cafeteria.
✉ **5 Mendele Street** ☎ **(03) 522 9141, fax (03) 522 9144**

City (£)
Near to the beach and centre of the city, this hotel offers utilitarian convenience without expensive frills.
✉ **9 Mapu Streeet** ☎ **(03) 524 6253, fax (03) 524 6250**

Dan Panorama (£££)
Isolated from the rest of the hotels in Tel Aviv, the Dan offers the best value of the largest hotels. Close to Jaffa and the business district.
✉ **10 Kaufmann Street**
☎ **(03) 519 0124; fax: (03) 517 1777**

Dan Tel Aviv (£££)
Most people's first choice for comfort, service and convenience. This large hotel has excellent facilities and splendid sea views.
✉ **99 HaYarkon Street**
☎ **(03) 520 2525**

Hilton (£££)
The city's most fashionable hotel and hang-out for the local high society. This is a large hotel located in the northern part of the hotel district.
✉ **Independence Park**
☎ **(03) 520 2222; fax: (03) 527 2711**

Metropolitan (££)
This comfortable but otherwise ordinary high-rise hotel is well located for the beach and centre of the city.
✉ **11/15 Trumpledor Street**
☎ **(03) 519 2727; fax: (03) 517 2626**

Sheraton (£££)
In the heart of the hotel district and overlooking the sea, the Sheraton challenges the Hilton's claim to be the city's premier hotel.
✉ **115 HaYarkon Street**
☎ **(03) 521 1111; fax: (03) 523 3322**

Eilat & the South

Beersheba
Paradise (££)
This modern hotel offers luxury accommodation by the city's standards. Stay over on a Wednesday night to get to the Bedouin market early Thursday morning.

✉ 4 Henrietta Szold Street ☎ (08) 640 5444; fax: (08) 640 5445

Dead Sea
Hyatt Regency Dead Sea Resort and Spa Hotel (£££)
This is the largest hotel in the region and offers medical treatment based on the sea's unique mineral contents, and a range of restaurants and recreational facilities.

✉ En Boqeq ☎ (08) 659 1234; fax: (08) 636 8811

Tsell Harim (£)
Comfortable and relatively cheap, this hotel, built in utilitarian 1960s style, is very near to the sea amid the hotel complex in En Boqeq.

✉ En Boqeq ☎ (08) 668 8100; fax: (08) 668 8111

Eilat
Etzion (£)
Far from the beach – and therefore cheaper – but situated conveniently close to the bus station, this hotel is ideal for budget travellers.

✉ 1 HaTamarim St ☎ (08) 637 0003; fax: (08) 637 0002

King Solomon's Palace (£££)
Stylish hotel with pleasant atmosphere and pleasing design overlooking the marina near the North Beach, an area that attracts a lot of nightbirds. Try the excellent buffet restaurant.

✉ North Beach ☎ (08) 636 3444; fax: (08) 633 4189

Lagoona (££)
More modestly priced than its sister hotel, King Solomon's Palace, but just as stylish. Both hotels, as well as the nearby Royal Beach and Sport, are owned by the British-based Isrotel group.

✉ North Beach ☎ (08) 636 6666; fax: (08) 633 2089

Moon Valley (£)
Far from the sea (a 10–15 minute walk) but the hotel does have its own swimming pool. Otherwise clean, comfortable but generally nondescript.

✉ North Beach ☎ (08) 637 3171; fax: (08) 637 1705

Princess (£££)
Far from the madding crowd and packed beaches in the centre of town, right by the Egyptian border at Taba, this is luxurious self-contained complex of restaurants and swimming pools.

✉ Near Taba border ☎ (08) 636 5555; fax: (08) 637 6333

Red Sea Sport Club Hotel (£)
Small and comfortable and the place to stay if you want to go scuba diving. Located opposite the quieter Coral Beach to the south of the city, the hotel runs week-long courses for divers.

✉ Coral Beach ☎ (08) 638 2222; fax: (08) 638 2200

Mizpé-Ramon
Ramon Inn (££)
A location for the adventurous in the heart of the desert near the Ramon Crater. The hotel is actually a converted block of flats.

✉ 1 Ein Akev ☎ (08) 658 8822; fax: (08) 658 8151

Youth Hostels
There is no shortage of youth hostels in city centres, although many of them are rather seedy. Representatives will often solicit backpackers at central bus stations. However, the Israel Youth Hostels Association (IYHA) has a nationwide network of hostels, offering excellent accommodation in both city centres and attractive locations in the Galilee and Negev.

✉ IYHA, POB 1075, Jerusalem ☎ (02) 655 8400; fax: (02) 655 8430. For camping information ✉ Israel Chalets and Camping Union, 112 Mishmar Street, Tel Aviv ☎ (03) 960 4524.

Department Stores, Malls & Markets

Exports
It is forbidden to export antiquities from Israel unless a written export permit (issued by the Department of Antiquities and Museums of the Ministry of Education and Culture) is provided with the goods.

Any consumer complaints should be addressed to the Ministry of Industry & Trade's Consumer Protection Service, 76 Mazeh Street, Tel Aviv ☎ (03) 710 1515.

Many stores geared to tourists will provide the receipts necessary to claim back the 17 per cent VAT on purchases of more than $50, at the airport. (This does not include tobacco products, electrical appliances, cameras, film or other photographic supplies). There is no VAT in Eilat.

There are duty free stores at Ben Gurion International and Eilat airports and many items, such as alcohol, tend to be cheaper there than at equivalent stores in Western Europe.

Department Stores

Jerusalem
Hamashbir LeZarchan
Israel's largest national chain of department stores is the place to go to find everything that you want under one roof, from stationery and clothing to perfume and electronics. There is also a branch in the Malkah Mall.

✉ **28 King George Street**
☎ **(02) 624 0511**
✉ **Malkah Shopping Mall**
☎ **(02) 679 3261**

Kravitz
Relatively small and intimate department store in downtown Jerusalem.
✉ **1 Ben Yehuda Street**
☎ **(02) 625 7433**

Galilee & the North

Haifa
Hamashbir LeZarchan
Apart from this outlet in Haifa, there are also branches in Kiriat Bialik, the Horev Centre, Karmi'el and Nahariya.
✉ **1 Yona Street, Hadar**
☎ **(04) 862 0936**

Tel Aviv & the Central Region

Tel Aviv
Hamashbir LeZarchan
See description on previous column. There are also branches in Allenby Street and in Rishon le-Ziyyon as well as at Ramat Gan and Ramit Aviv.
✉ **Dizengoff Centre** ☎ **03 528 5136**

Eilat & the South

Eilat
Hamashbir LeZarchan
See description in previous column.
✉ **Tamarim Street** ☎ **(08) 637 2102**

Shopping Malls

Jerusalem
Kanion Ahim Israel
Modest-sized shopping mall in the large shopping centre in the Talpiot Industrial Zone.
✉ **18 Yad Haruzim Street**
☎ **(02) 673 3923**

Kanion Jerusalem
Situated adjacent to the municipal soccer stadium, this is the largest shopping mall in Israel. It houses, among other things, department stores, clothes shops, shoe shops, gift shops, cinemas, restaurants, cafés and fast-food outlets. There is air-conditioned comfort in the summer and heating in the winter. Convenient and comfortable – but one could be anywhere in the world.
✉ **Malkah** ☎ **(02) 679 1333**
🕐 **Sun–Thu 9:30–9, Fri9:30–2:30, Sat 1hr after sunset–11PM**
🚌 **31, 6**

Galilee & the North

Haifa
Merkaz Horev
The city's leading shopping mall, on top of Mount Carmel.
✉ 15 Horev Street ☎ (04) 824 6164

Tel Aviv & the Central Region

Tel Aviv
Dizengoff Centre
The city's slightly shabby, most centrally located shopping mall.
✉ 50 Dizengoff Street ☎ (03) 525 8351

Kanion Hazahav
The industrial area south of Tel Aviv, in Rishon le-Ziyyon, is Israel's consumer capital, and Kanion Hazahav is the largest of the many shopping centres in the area.
✉ 21 Sakharov Street, New Industrial Zone, Rishon le-Ziyyon ☎ (03) 962 2678

Eilat & the South

Beersheba
Kanion HaNegev
The largest shopping mall in the south can be found just north of the Bedouin market in Beersheba.
✉ Eli Cohen junction, Beersheba ☎ (08) 628 1222

Markets

Jerusalem
Arab Souk
Located in the Muslim quarter of the Old City these bustling, narrow alleyways are packed with religious souvenirs, T-shirts, ceramics, spices and everything the tourist might want.

Mahane Yehuda
The place to come to for fruit and vegetables, nuts and pickles, fish and meat and an appetizing range of other foodstuffs. If not to buy, come just to savour the atmosphere.

Galilee & the North

Daliyat El-Karmel
Some 15 kilometres southeast of Haifa, this Druse village is popular for its market, which offers ceramics and earthenware, clothes and religious items.

Tel Aviv & the Central Region

Tel Aviv
Carmel Market
Israel's largest market offers fresh fruit and vegetables as well as clothes and all manner of other bargains. Stretching between Allenby Street and the seafront, this market probably offers the best and widest choice of bargains in Israel.

Flea Market
Located off Yefet Street in Jaffa this market specializes in antiques and general bric-à-brac. It's best to get there in the morning.

Eilat & the South

Beersheba
Bedouin Market
Open only on Thursday mornings, this market sells everything from fruit and vegetables to clothing. The greatest pleasure is not so much to buy but to see the Bedouin, the market's original customers, haggling over the price of a camel or goat.

How to Haggle
If you're not the type to get embarrassed then haggling in the Arab *souk* can be fun. Always pay a fraction of the initial asking price. Never rush into anything and the more disinterested you seem, the lower the price will come. Almost nothing is unique and dozens of stores carry the same items. Check out how much the items you covet cost in the fixed-price stores of west Jerusalem, and then aim to lower it in the *souk*. Enjoy the experience. For more expensive items shopkeepers will make you a cup of coffee while you sit down and negotiate.

Books, Maps &
Fashion

Newspapers and Magazines

In addition to the leading newspapers and magazines from Western Europe, visitors may wish to purchase the *Jerusalem Post*, Israel's oldest daily English language daily, as well as the *International Herald Tribune*, printed daily in Tel Aviv along with an English translation of the *Ha'aretz* newspaper. Both papers are issued six times a week (not Saturdays) and have an expanded Friday edition. Also worth reading is the *Jerusalem Report*, a bi-weekly magazine covering Israel, the Middle East and the Jewish world.

Books & Maps

Feldheim
Excellent selection of Jewish holy books and books about Judaism in English.
- ✉ 9 Strauss Street, Jerusalem
- ☎ (02) 538 6779

Memsi
Good selection of maps and tour guides.
- ✉ 31 Ben Yehuda Street, Jerusalem ☎ (02) 625 0661
- ✉ 20 Harekevet Street, Tel Aviv ☎ (03) 564 1122

Steimatsky
This nationwide chain of book stores and newsagents stocks a range of foreign and local newspapers, as well as novels and travel guides printed in English. Branches can be found in almost every city centre and shopping mall (the main ones are listed below). In Downtown Jerusalem alone there are four branches, the largest being just east of Zion Square. In Tel Aviv, the Allenby Street branch is the largest in the whole chain, with two floors of books in English. Other outlets in Tel Aviv can be found in the Dizengoff Centre, the New Central Bus Station, the Hilton Hotel and the Kanion Ayalon shopping mall.

- ✉ 39 Jaffa Road, Jerusalem ☎ (02) 625 0155
- ✉ 16 Herzl Street, Hadar, Haifa ☎ (04) 866 5042
- ✉ 12 Hagalil Street, Tiberias ☎ (04) 679 1288
- ✉ 71 Allenby Street, Tel Aviv ☎ (03) 528 1187

- ✉ Central Bus Station, Eilat ☎ (08) 637 5084

Fashion

Jerusalem
Castro
Leading chain for women's casual fashions. There is also a branch in Mevasseret Zion.
- ✉ 18 King George St. ☎ 02 625 5421

Roberto
Jerusalem fashion chain for men. Also has a branch in the Jerusalem Canion in Malkah.
- ✉ 58 Jaffa Road ☎ (02) 624 7098

Galilee & the North

Haifa
Benetton
Franchise of the famous Italian chain.
- ✉ 109 Hanassi Boulevard ☎ (04) 837 3190

Tel Aviv & the Central Region

Beged Or
The place to buy leather fashions. More branches in Jerusalem and Haifa.
- ✉ Opera Tower, 1 Allenby Street ☎ (03) 510 7096

Lady Polgat
The women's half of the Polgat fashion chain. This branch is located in fashionable Gan Ha'Ir, by Rabin Square.
- ✉ 71 Ibn Gbriol Street ☎ (03) 527 9162

Polgat
Fashion chain for men located in Gan Ha'Ir by Rabin Square.
- ✉ 71 Ibn Gbriol Street ☎ (03) 527 9162

Gifts

Souvenirs

Jerusalem

Arieh Klein
This warehouse has the best choice of olive wood items.
✉ **3 Ziv Yosef Street (off Bar Ilan Street), Sanhedria** ☎ **(02) 538 9992**

Hatzofrim
Judaica and Jewish ritual items in silver. Part of a nationwide chain – there is also a branch in Geula near Me'a She'arim.
✉ **5 Kanfei Nesharim, Shatner Centre, Givat Sha'ul** ☎ **(02) 651 4026**

Jerusalem House of Quality
Contains a range of stores selling antiquities and Judaica. Also try Hutzot Hayotzer, opposite the Jaffa Gate.
✉ **12 Hebron Street (opposite Mount Zion Hotel)** ☎ **(02) 672 5111**

Karakashian Armenian Pottery
Tasteful tiles and pottery that make great gifts. Allow a few days to order personalised tiles.
✉ **Via Dolorosa, near the sixth Station** ☎ **(02) 626 1587**

Tel Aviv & the Central Region

Gordon Street
Running from the seafront by the Sheraton Hotel through to Dizengoff, this street is home to dozens of art galleries and gift shops.

Nahalat Binyamin
Stretching south to east from the corner of Allenby and King George Streets, there is a jewellery market in this pedestrian mall Tuesdays and Fridays as well as many souvenir shops.

Eilat & the South

Eilat

Coral World Underwater Observatory
The store here has coral gifts and other items relating to Red Sea marine life.
✉ **Coral Beach** ☎ **(08) 636 4200**

G.R.A.S.
Part of a nationwide chain selling pottery and gifts.
✉ **14 Mul Hayam Shopping Centre** ☎ **(08) 632 6941**

Diamonds

Jerusalem

National Diamond Centre
Israel is the world's largest centre for cutting and polishing diamonds and this is the largest national retail chain.
✉ **143 Bethlehem Street** ☎ **(02) 673 3770**

Galilee & the North

Haifa

M Miller Jewellery
The city's leading diamond specialist.
✉ **50 Herzl Street** ☎ **(04) 866 6612**

Tel Aviv & the Central Region

Tel Aviv

National Diamond Centre
This, and the surrounding stores by the Diamond Exchange, is the place to come if you are looking for the best choice and bargains.
✉ **Room 1645, Maccabbee Building, Diamond Exchange, Ramat Gan** ☎ **(03) 575 3404**

What to Buy

Nothing is especially cheaper in Israel than elsewhere except for leatherware and diamonds. Above and beyond items of religious and ritual use, uniquely Holy Land gifts include olive wood carvings (which, with their attractive light and dark grains, are both aesthetically pleasing and have sentimental religious significance), Hebron glassware, copper and brassware (including coffee trays), ceramics and earthenware. Also available are T-shirts with a range of Hebrew, Arabic and English slogans related to Israel.

Children's Attractions

Food for the Fussy
As throughout the Mediterranean, so in Israel children are conspicuously indulged. Israelis, whether Jews or Arabs, dote on children so don't worry about all that noise and mess. Fast food restaurants actually cater for children, but other eateries rarely have special menus. However, staff are frequently only too happy to pander to your child's every whim. Children generally love being able to tuck food into the pocket of a pitta bread.

Jerusalem
With all that religion and history Jerusalem can be heavy going for children. Nevertheless, the Old City, with its bustling narrow alleyways, noise, colour and smell of spices, can be very exotic and exciting (and scary) for children large and small alike. Try a camel ride at the Mount of Olives lookout or visit some of the city's excellent child-friendly museums.

Biblical Zoo (Tisch Family Zoological Gardens)
Built attractively into the hillside in Malkah, this zoo specialises in the animals of the Bible, with exhibits that include relevant Bible quotations. The complex includes a playground and petting corner.
✉ **Gan Hakhayot Street, Malkah** 🕐 **Sun–Thu 9–7:30 (5PM in winter), Fri and day before public hols 9–3, Sat 10–6:30 (5PM in winter)** 🚌 **26**

Bloomfield Science Museum
This museum has excellent hands-on exhibits (➤ 40).

Ein Yael Living Museum
Here children can create their own mosaics, practise ancient crafts and plant their own crops.
✉ **Nakhal Refaim, Malkah** 🕐 **Daily 9–4; hands-on activities only on Sat, public holidays and throughout Aug**

Israel Museum
Visit the excellent hands-on youth wing (➤ 20).

Liberty Bell Garden
The park can be found between King David and Jabotinsky Streets, and has excellent play facilities and a puppet theatre in a railway carriage.
🚌 **4, 5, 6, 7, 18, 21, 30**

Galilee & the North
If your children enjoy travelling in cars and buses and taking in the scenery this region can be fun for them. If not, then steer clear of the Galilee. The northern Mediterranean coastline has excellent beaches but beware the ostensibly calm sea's strong undercurrents. There are water parks at Kibbutz Neve Yam, 14km south of Haifa, and at Tsemakh at the Sea of Galilee's most southerly point.

Carmelit
This is a fun way of travelling up and down Haifa's hillsides. This six station subway system is actually an underground cable-car.

Haifa Cable-Car
Near the Central Bus Station at the southern entrance to the city, the cable-car offers a fun view of sea and city.

Rosh HaNikra Caves
Children often enjoy the cable-car trip and the underground network of caves (➤ 63).

Israel National Museum of Science
This excellent museum has hands-on exhibits that are most appropriate for older children (➤ 53).
✉ **Balfour Street , Haifa** ☎ **(04) 682 8111** 🕐 **Sun, Mon, Wed, Thu 9–6, Tue 9–7:30, Fri 10–3, Sat 10–5.**

Tel Aviv & the Central Region

Tel Aviv and other Mediterranean resorts such as Ashkelon, Herzliyya and Netanya, mean golden beaches with strategically placed ice-cream kiosks. There are also excellent water parks at Shefayim (☎ (09) 959 5757), just north of Herzliyya, and Ashqeluna (☎ (07) 673 9970) near Ashkelon.

Kfar Daniel Monkey Park

A well-designed park that gives the impression that the visitors are in captivity while the monkeys roam free.

✉ **Kfar Daniel (near the airport)** ☎ (08) 928 5888 🕐 **Daily 9–4** 🚌 21

Lunar Park

All the fun of the fair in Israel's largest fairground.

✉ **Rokach Boulevard, Tel Aviv** ☎ (03) 642 7080 🕐 **Open Sat and school holidays 10:30–5** 🚌 47, 48

Safari Park

Children will see mainly African animals, including lions and giraffes, at this zoo complex. Café on site.

✉ **Safari Park, Ramat Gan** ☎ (03) 674 4981 🕐 **Oct–May, Sat–Thu 9–2:30, Fri 9–2; Jun–Sep, Sat–Thu 9–5, Fri 9–1** 🚌 35

Eilat & the South

The unique experience of floating in the Dead Sea and the brilliant display of fish in the Red Sea should appeal to most children.

Coral World

There's lots to do here for children, who will especially love looking out into 'the deep' from the safety of the underwater observatory (➤ 18).

✉ **Coral Beach, Eilat** ☎ (08) 636 4200 🕐 **Sat–Thu 8:30–4:30 (5PM Apr–Oct), Fri & eve of festivals 8:30–3. Closed Yom Kippur** 🚌 15

Dolphin Reef

There are training and feeding sessions each hour for the dolphins and sea lions, and it is possible to swim and dive in the water with them too.

✉ **Southern Beach, Eilat** ☎ (08) 637 1846 🕐 **Daily 9–5** 🚌 15

Hay Bar Nature Reserve

Youngsters will enjoy the animals and the 'nasties' in the predators zoo (➤ 85).

✉ **35km north of Eilat** ☎ (08) 637 6018 🕐 **Tours daily at 10, 11, 12, 1, 2, 3**

Masada

Children will enjoy the cable-car ride up to the Roman fort ruins at the top of Mount Masada, and the view, if not the archaeology.

☎ (08) 658 4207 🕐 **Apr–Oct daily 8–4, Nov–Mar daily 8–3**

Texas Ranch

Lawrence of Arabia meets Billy the Kid. This Wild West town was originally built as a movie set. Horse, pony and camel rides are available as well as Bedouin meals in an authentic tent.

✉ **Opposite Eilat Port** ☎ (08) 637 6663 🕐 **daily 8–5** 🚌 15

Qalya

A swimming pool and water park handily situated on the northern shore of the Dead Sea.

☎ (02) 994 2393 🕐 **daily 9–5** 🚌 421, 444

Children's Reductions

Children under five travel free on the buses but older ones pay full fare. In museums children under four usually enter free and half price is charged for youngsters aged 4–18.

In cars (except taxis) children under four must by law be fixed into child seats.

The Arts

Musical Greats

Many of the world's finest musicians began their careers in Israel, including violinists Yitzhak Perlman and Pinchas Zuckerman as well as pianist and conductor Daniel Barenboim, who all first appeared with the Israel Philharmonic Orchestra (IPO). Indian-born maestro Zubin Mehta has been the director of music for the IPO since 1968.

Theatre

Israelis are very proud of their theatre and claim to have the highest per capita number of theatre-goers in the world. Unfortunately, most theatre is in Hebrew although simultaneous translations are sometimes available. Occasionally there are top-quality productions touring from overseas, especially during the Israel Festival (May/June). Israeli theatre encompasses translations from world drama as well as original Hebrew productions, which tend to be very politicised. dealing with issues of war and peace, social tensions and the Holocaust.

Jerusalem

Jerusalem Theatre

The capital's principal theatre does not have a company of its own but showcases the best of Israeli theatre and productions from around the world. It forms part of the Jerusalem Centre for Performing Arts complex, which includes theatres and concert halls.
✉ 20 Marcus Street, ☎ (02) 560 5757 🚌 15

Khan Theatre

Located in a converted 19th-century warehouse, this theatre frequently features fringe productions.
✉ David Remez Street ☎ (02) 671 8281 🚌 4, 5, 6, 7, 8, 14, 21

Galilee & the North

Haifa Municipal Theatre

Home of the Haifa Theatre Company.

✉ 50 Pvazner Street, Haifa ☎ (04) 862 0670 🚇 Carmelit: Gan Ha'Em Station

Tel Aviv & the Central Region

Carmeri Theatre

The home of one of Israel's leading theatre companies.
✉ 101 Dizengoff Street, Tel Aviv ☎ (03) 523 3335 🚌 5

Habimah Theatre

Home of Israel's national theatre company (➤ 70).
✉ Habimah Square, Tel Aviv ☎ (03) 527 3740 🚌 5

Eilat & the South

Beersheba Municipal Theatre

This is the home of a dynamic, young repertory company that tours the country as well as showing the best of Israeli theatre.
✉ Bet Ha'am, Zalman Shazar, Beersheba ☎ (08) 623 8278

Music

Israel has several world-class orchestras, including the Israel Philharmonic Orchestra and the Jerusalem Symphony Orchestra.

Jerusalem

Henry Crown Hall

Part of the Jerusalem Centre for the Performing Arts, this is the home of the Jerusalem Symphony Orchestra.
✉ Chopin Street ☎ (02) 561 7167 🚌 15

Pargod Theatre

Cellar setting for jazz and folk performances.
✉ 94 Bezalel Street ☎ (02) 623 1765 🚌 19

Tel Aviv & the Central Region

Bet Lessing
Jazz, folk and theatre performances.
✉ **34 Weizman Boulevard, Tel Aviv** ☎ **(03) 694 1111** 🚌 **7**

Mann Auditorium
Home of the Israel Philharmonic Orchestra.
✉ **11 Dizengoff Street, Tel Aviv** ☎ **(03) 528 9163** 🚌 **5**

Tel Aviv Centre for the Performing Arts
Home of the New Israel Opera (► 71). Concerts are frequently given here by the Rishon le-Ziyyon Symphony Orchestra.
✉ **28 Leonardo Da Vinci Street, Tel Aviv** ☎ **(03) 692 7707** 🚌 **18, 32, 70**

Dance

Israeli dance troupes uniquely combine Western and Eastern styles with biblical and contemporary themes. All the major dance companies are based in Tel Aviv but perform around the country in the aforementioned theatres.

Tel Aviv

Bat Dor Dance Company
✉ **30 Ibn Gbriol Street, Tel Aviv** ☎ **(03) 696 3178** 🚌 **5**

Batsheva Dance Company and Inbal Dance Company
Both based at the Suzanne Delal Centre.
✉ **6 Yechieli Street, Neve Tzedek, Tel Aviv** ☎ **(03) 510 5656**

Israel Ballet
✉ **2 Hay Be'er Street, Tel Aviv** ☎ **(03) 696 6610**

Kol U'Demama (Sound and Silence)
A unique troop of deaf and hard of hearing dancers, who are able to base their routines on the vibrations of the floor.
✉ **81 HaYarkon Street, Tel Aviv** ☎ **(03) 510 2997**

Cinema

Israeli cinemas show all the Hollywood blockbusters as well as the pick of the latest movies from all over the world. These films usually have English subtitles, but check at the box office. Jerusalem, Tel Aviv and Haifa have cinematheque clubs (► below), where film buffs see the best of world cinema through the ages; these are great places to catch up on golden oldies. Israel itself makes a dozen movies a year which are screened with English subtitles. These are generally not great cinema but offer an interesting window into Israeli culture.
Information on performances can be found in the two English-language daily newspapers – *The Jerusalem Post* and *Ha'aretz/ International Herald Tribune* or at ticket agencies.

Jerusalem Cinematheque
✉ **Hebron Street** ☎ **(02) 672 4131** 🚌 **5, 6, 7, 21**

Haifa Cinematheque
✉ **142 Hanassi Boulevard** ☎ **(04) 838 3424** 🚇 **Carmelit: Gan Ha'Em Station**

Tel Aviv Cinematheque
✉ **2 Sprinza Street** ☎ **(03) 691 7181**

Inspiring Venues
If possible it is worth taking in an outdoor performance at the Sultan's Pool, romantically located beneath Jerusalem's Old City walls, or the Caesarea Amphitheatre, which has the Mediterranean as a backdrop lapping gently against the shore. Check with ticket agents.

Nightlife

Get Going Late
If you go out on the town in Israel you may be surprised to find places are very quiet, as Israel's nightlife, especially for the young, does not get going until after midnight. Israelis are not big alcohol drinkers and tend to nurse one drink all night. Drunkenness is viewed very negatively.

Jerusalem
Jerusalem's nightlife is surprisingly lively. The busiest cafés and restaurants are in the pedestrian precincts of Ben Yehuda and Nahalat Shiva, but later in the night the action moves to the pubs in the Russian Compound's Monbaz and Hamalkah Streets. The Talpiot Industrial Zone to the southeast of the city is home to many of the larger nightclubs and discos, while the grander hotels have more exclusive and expensive nightclubs.

Glasnost
The busiest of the Russian Compound pubs.
✉ **15 Heleni Hamalkah Street** ☎ **(02) 625 6954**

Haoman 17
One of Israel's best-known clubs.
✉ **17 Haoman Street** ☎ **(02) 678 1658**

Hataasia
Pleasant decor with two dance floors.
✉ **5 Hataasia Street** ☎ **(02) 673 7311**

Shonka
A dance bar with restaurant.
✉ **1 Hasoreg Street** ☎ **(02) 625 7033**

Galilee & the North
Nightlife in Haifa is concentrated in the Hadar midtown district and Central Carmel. Outside Haifa, this essentially rural region has little to offer in the way of nightlife.

Jaoa
Great dance bar in the Galilee.
✉ **Ramat Yishai** ☎ **(04) 953 0076**

Tel Aviv & the Central Region
Tel Aviv proudly boasts that it is the city that never stops, and to be sure the place is busy well into the small hours. The seafront, Dizengoff and Jaffa port are busy while Schenkin and Florentin are the trendy districts.

Fetish
Popular dance bar with plenty of energy and atmosphere.
✉ **14 Rambam Street** ☎ **(03) 510 8807**

Octopus
One of the city's largest dance floors.
✉ **Tel Aviv Port** ☎ **(03) 620 2348**

Scene
Small and crowded dance bar.
✉ **56 Allenby Street** ☎ **(03) 510 8523**

Eilat & the South
Eilat has a lively night scene, mostly focused around the tourist centre by the North Beach and the promenade along the marina.

Bura-Bura
As good as any place to dance away the night.
✉ **Dalia Hotel, North Beach** ☎ **(07) 633 0469**

C-Bar
Lively dance bar popular with the 25 plus crowd.
✉ **Ophira Park** ☎ **(08) 633 4423**

Sports

Diving & Sea Sports

Sea sports, especially scuba diving, are the activities most worth pursuing in Israel, especially to see the remarkable Red Sea marine life. In the Mediterranean, archaeological diving is very popular, with several dozen wrecks at the bottom of the sea from Byzantine times onwards tempting divers. Contact:

✉ **The Federation for Underwater Activities, POB 6110, Tel Aviv 61060** ☎ **(03) 546 7968**

Equipment can be hired from the places listed below; the first three also arrange waterskiing, windsurfing and boardsurfing.

Lucky Divers
✉ Radisson Moriah Hotel, North Beach, Eilat ☎ (08) 637 5935

Red Sea Divers
✉ Red Sea Sport Hotel, Coral Beach, Eilat ☎ (08) 638 2222

Octopus Diving School
✉ Tel Aviv Marina ☎ (03) 527 1440

Ze'ev Hayam Diving Club
✉ 71 Yerushalim Street, Haifa ☎ (04) 832 3911

River Sports

Inner-tubing down the River Jordan
Kibbutz Sde Nehemya
☎ (06) 694 6010

Katarafting
Kibbutz Kfar Hanassi
☎ (06) 691 4992;

Kayaking
Kibbutz Kfar Blum
☎ (06) 694 8657

Snapelling/Rock climbing
Kibbutz Mizpé Shalem
☎ (02) 994 5111

Skiing

Mount Hermon Ski Site
✉ Neve Ativ, Golan Heights
☎ (06) 698 1339; for accommodation ☎ (04) 698 1331

Horse Riding

Kind David Stables
✉ Neve Ilan, Judean Hills
☎ (02) 534 0535

Vered HaGalil Ranch
✉ Korazim, Upper Galilee
☎ (04) 673 5785

Parachuting

Sky Club
✉ Moshav HaBonim (between Tel Aviv and Haifa) ☎ (04) 639 1068

Spectator Sports

Owing to political boycotts Israeli teams compete in Europe rather than Asia. Israel's soccer teams seldom make much impact in the European Cup championships, but the Maccabi Tel Aviv basketball team has twice won the European Cup.

Soccer

Betar Jerusalem
✉ Teddy Stadium, Malkah, Jerusalem ☎ (02) 678 8376

Maccabi Tel Aviv
✉ Maccabi Stadium, Tel Aviv
☎ (03) 604 7230

Basketball

Maccabi Tel Aviv
✉ Yad Eliahu, Tel Aviv
☎ (03) 527 2112

The Maccabiah

Held once every four years in Israel, the Maccabiah is the Jewish Olympics. The 15th Maccabiah in 1997 drew 5,500 competitors to Israel from 54 countries worldwide to compete in over 50 different sports. The Maccabiah is the world's third largest sporting event after the Olympics and the World Student Games and one of only seven events under the auspices of the International Olympic Committee (IOC). The 16th Maccabiah will be held on 16–26 July 2001.

What's On When

Jewish and Muslim Calendars

The Jewish calendar follows a lunar-solar cycle. There are 12 lunar months each year with a 'leap month' added every two to three years in line with the solar year. Thus Jewish festivals can vary up to a month in the Gregorian calendar. Besides religious festivals, Israelis use the Gregorian calendar. The Jewish day lasts from sunset to sunset, so that the sabbath is from sunset on Friday to sunset on Saturday.

The Muslim calendar is lunar with 12 months a year. Festivals rotate backwards through the Gregorian calendar. Principal festivals are *New Year*, *Mohammed's Birthday*, *Ramadan* (a month long fast from sunrise to sunset), *Id el Fitr* (conclusion of Ramadan) and *Id el Adkha* (Feast of the Sacrifice).

Jan/Feb

Orthodox Christmas: the Orthodox community celebrates Christmas on 6 Jan.
Tu B'Shvat: the Jewish New Year for trees is marked with planting ceremonies around the country.

Mar/Apr

Purim: a carnival-style festival with fancy dress to celebrate the saving of Persian Jews from extermination in the biblical book of Esther.
Jerusalem International Book Fair: held biennially in Jerusalem.
Pesach (Passover): recalls the exodus from Egypt. During the week-long festival no bread is eaten or available.
Easter: usually concurrent with Passover (the Last Supper was the Passover meal), the highlight is the Good Friday procession on the Via Dolorosa.

May/Jun

Holocaust Day: to commemorate the six million Jews who perished in the Holocaust; all places of entertainment are closed.
Memorial Day: the day before Independence Day is dedicated to the soldiers who have fallen in Israel's wars. Once again places of entertainment are closed.
Independence Day: merrymakers hit each other with the (plastic) hammer of freedom.
Lag B'Omer: Israel's bonfire night celebrates a range of miracles.
Shavuot (Pentecost): harvest festival celebrating the giving of the Torah to the Jews on Mount Sinai.

Israel Festival: the country's biggest cultural event with theatre and dance from around the world takes place in Jerusalem.

Jul/Aug

Jerusalem Film Festival: movies shown from around the world.
Tisha B'Av: all places of entertainment are closed during this fast to commemorate the destruction of the Temple.
Tu B'Av: marks the beginning of the grape harvest. Also known as the Lovers' Festival.
Karmiel Dance Festival: held in the Galilee in July.
Jaffa Nights: series of free outdoor concerts in August.

Sep/Oct

Rosh Hashanah: two-day public holiday for the Jewish New Year.
Yom Kippur: the holiest day of the year. A 25-hour period of fasting and prayer as the country literally comes to a standstill.
Succot (Tabernacles): Jews build small wooden huts to dine in to recall the 40 years wandering in the Sinai. The last day, *Simchat Torah*, marks the beginning of the Torah cycle.
'Akko Fringe Theatre Festival: Israel's leading fringe festival is held during *Succot*.

Nov/Dec

Chanukah: eight-day festival of lights to commemorate the Hasmonean victory over the Greeks and the rededication of the Temple.
Christmas: the focus of attention is Manger Square in Bethlehem.

Practical Matters

TIME DIFFERENCES

GMT 12 noon	Israel 2PM	Germany 1PM	USA (NY) 7AM	Netherlands 1PM	Spain 1PM
	→	→	←	→	→

BEFORE YOU GO

WHAT YOU NEED

- ● Required
- ▲ Not required

	UK	Germany	USA	Netherlands	Spain
Passport/National Identity Card	●	●	●	●	●
Visa (routinely granted at point of entry into Israel)	●	●	●	●	●
Onward or return ticket	▲	▲	▲	▲	▲
Health inoculations (recommended: hepatitis A, polio and typhoid)	▲	▲	▲	▲	▲
Health documentation – reciprocal agreements	▲	▲	▲	▲	▲
Travel insurance	●	●	●	●	●
Driving licence (national with English translation or international)	●	●	●	●	●
Insurance documents (hire car)	●	●	●	●	●
Car registration document (hire car)	●	●	●	●	●

WHEN TO GO

Jerusalem

High season

Low season

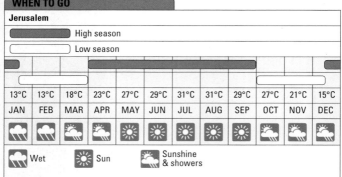

JAN	FEB	MAR	APR	MAY	JUN	JUL	AUG	SEP	OCT	NOV	DEC
13°C	13°C	18°C	23°C	27°C	29°C	31°C	31°C	29°C	27°C	21°C	15°C

🌧️ Wet   ☀️ Sun   🌦️ Sunshine & showers

TOURIST OFFICES

In the UK
Israel Government
Tourist Office
180 Oxford Street
London W1N 9DJ
☎ (0171) 299 1111
Fax: (0171) 299 1112

In the USA
Israel Government
Tourist Office
19th Floor, 350 Fifth
Avenue, New York
NY 10118
☎ (212) 560 0600
Fax: (212) 629 4368

Internet tourist information:
http://www.israel-mfa.gov.il/sites.html

POLICE 100

FIRE 102

AMBULANCE 101

OTHER CRISIS LINES – See local phone book

WHEN YOU ARE THERE

ARRIVING

Most visitors to Israel land at Ben Gurion International Airport. There are daily flights by Israel's national airline, El Al, from major North American and European cities as well as many destinations in the Far East. El Al also flies directly to Uvda near Eilat.

Ben Gurion International Airport	Journey Times
Kilometres to Tel Aviv	N/A
	25 minutes
15 kilometres	25 minutes

Ben Gurion International Airport	Journey times
Kilometres to Jerusalem	N/A
	45 minutes
44 kilometres	45 minutes

MONEY

The monetary unit of Israel is the New Israeli Shekel, (NIS) which is divided into 100 agorot (single – agora). Coins come in 5,10 and 50 agorot, 1, 5 and 10 shekels. There are 20, 50, 100 and 200 NIS notes. Major credits cards are accepted everywhere and bank cash machines will dispense shekels against them. Banks and change bureaux will accept all foreign currencies and travellers' cheques.

TIME

Israel is two hours ahead of GMT (GMT+2). Daylight saving time (when the clock is moved one hour forward) operates between late March and early September.

CUSTOMS

YES

There are specific allowances of alcohol, cigarettes, perfumes and gifts into the country for those over 18 years of age:
Alcohol, spirits: 1 litre
Wine: 2 litres
Cigarettes: 250 or
Tobacco products:
  250 grams
Perfume or toilet water:
  0.25 litres
Gifts must not exceed US$200 in value and expensive items (video cameras, laptop computers, jewellery) should be officially declared and a refundable deposit paid. Nowadays these regulations are rarely enforced except for conspicuous gifts such as TV sets or VCRs.
Unlimited amounts of currency can be brought in and out of Israel.

NO

Drugs, firearms, explosives, weapons and so on. Foods, plants and animals should be declared.

EMBASSIES AND CONSULATES

UK	**Germany**	**USA**	**Netherlands**	**Spain**
(02) 582 8281	(03) 693 1313	(02) 625 3288	(03) 695 7377	(02) 563 3473
(Jerusalem)	(Tel Aviv)	(Jerusalem)	(Tel Aviv)	(Jerusalem)

WHEN YOU ARE THERE

TOURIST OFFICES

- **'Akko**
  ✉ Al-Jazzar Street
  (opposite mosque)
  ☎ (04) 981 9926

- **Ben Gurion International Airport**
  ☎ (03) 971 1485 (in arrivals hall, open 24 hours)

- **Bethlehem**
  ✉ Manger Square
  ☎ (02) 274 1581

- **Eilat**
  ✉ Yotam Street, corner of Ha'arava Street
  ☎ (08) 637 2111

- **Jerusalem**
  ✉ 17 Jaffa Road
  ☎ (02) 625 8844

  ✉ Jaffa Gate
  ☎ (02) 628 0382

- **Nazareth**
  ✉ Casa Nova Street
  ☎ (04) 657 0555

- **Safed**
  ✉ Municipal Building
  ☎ (04) 692 7485

- **Tel Aviv**
  ✉ New Central Bus Station
  ☎ (03) 639 5660

- **Tiberias**
  ✉ Habanim Street
  ☎ (04) 672 5666

All these offices are individually run by their municipalities and have different opening times, but are typically open Sun–Thu 8:30–5, Fri 8:30–12.

JEWISH NATIONAL HOLIDAYS

J	F	M	A	M	J	J	A	S	O	N	D
		(1)	(1)	(2)	(1)			(1)	(1)	(1)	(1)

Mar/Apr	Passover (first and last days of seven-day festival)
Apr/May	Independence Day
	Yom Hashoah – Holocaust Day
	Yom Hazikaron – Memorial Day
May/June	Jerusalem Liberation Day
	Shavuot – Pentecost
Sep/Oct	Rosh Hashanah – Jewish New Year (two days)
	Yom Kippur – Day of Atonement
	Succot – Tabernacles (first and last days of eight-day festival)
Nov/Dec	Chanukah – Feast of Lights

Festivals, like the sabbath, last from sunset until sunset. In Arab areas stores and businesses are open on these national holidays but are closed on Muslim festivals.

OPENING HOURS

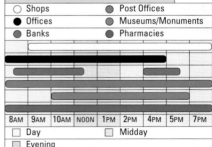

○ Shops	● Post Offices
● Offices	● Museums/Monuments
● Banks	● Pharmacies

☐ Day ☐ Midday ☐ Evening

Many shops are open until much later than the times shown. All shops close Friday afternoon and Saturday but some open Saturday night. In small towns some shops close 1–4. Muslim-owned shops are closed all day Friday and Christian-owned shops on Sunday. Read the *Jerusalem Post* to find out which pharmacy is on duty to open 24 hours. Opening times of museums, banks and post offices can vary but they are closed Friday afternoon and all day Saturday. Some offices may close for lunch and only receive the public in the morning.

DRIVE ON THE
RIGHT

TOILETS
BASIC

Usually free but sometimes a small fee is charged for the purchase of toilet paper.

PUBLIC TRANSPORT

Internal Flights There are airports in Eilat, Haifa, Herzliyya, Jerusalem, Rosh-Pinna and Tel Aviv. Arkia Israel Airlines runs regular internal flights (☎ (03) 699 2222) but as there is a good road system, little time is saved except on flights to Eilat.

Trains With exception of the Tel Aviv–Haifa line (some trains continuing north to Nahariya) Israel's train network is negligible. The daily Jerusalem–Tel Aviv train is worth taking for the scenic journey but takes two hours compared to 50 minutes taken by bus. There are no trains on Friday afternoon or Saturday. Train information ☎ (03) 577 4000. Haifa has a six-station underground train – the Carmelit. ☎ (04) 837 6861.

Buses Israel's public transport system revolves around the bus and the Egged Bus Cooperative is a national institution. Buses are comfortable and punctual but drivers go too fast. Multi-ride tickets and long intercity runs are good value. Egged information: Tel Aviv ☎ (03) 624 8888. Dan Information (for Tel Aviv region) ☎ (03) 639 4444.

Shared Taxis (*Sherutim*) These taxis (which carry up to seven people) charge similar fares to buses and travel the major intercity routes as well as some urban routes. They are the only avaliable transport on the sabbath and also run through the night after public transport has stopped.

CAR RENTAL

Rental cars, from small saloons to people-movers, are available at Ben Gurion International Airport and all major city locations. A range of major international companies, such as Hertz and Avis, have a national network in Israel alongside large local companies like Eldan. It is much cheaper to pre-book a car in your own country.

TAXIS

By law all taxis operate on a meter system. However, drivers will frequently offer a flat fare, which is probably higher than the meter would amount to, and is also a way of evading taxation. There is a surcharge for the trips made in the evening and on the sabbath.

DRIVING

Speed limit on motorways (blue signs) 90/100kph

Speed limit on highways (green signs) 80/90 kph

Speed limit on urban roads **50/60 kph**

It is compulsory for drivers and passengers in front and back seats to wear seat belts at all times.

Breath testing is very rarely carried out. The limit is 0.05 per cent of alcohol per litre or blood.

Petrol comes in leaded and unleaded grades (91, 96, 98 octane), and, like diesel, is sold by the litre. Fuel is generally cheaper than in Western Europe, but more expensive than in the US. Petrol stations are plentiful except in the Negev; all accept international credit cards.

If your rental car breaks down, you should contact the rental company, who will come and repair or replace the vehicle. Otherwise contact national breakdown services such as Shagrir ☎ (02) 625 3530.

CENTIMETRES

0 1 2 3 4 5 6 7 8

INCHES

0 1 2 3

PERSONAL SAFETY

Violent crime is relatively rare in Israel, although theft is rampant. The major threat is from terrorism — beware of unattended bags in crowded places.
• In Palestinian areas, it may be safer to travel by Arab bus or taxi rather than in an Israeli rental car, which can be easily identified by its yellow number plate.
• Hitch-hiking is very easy but there have been instances of hitch-hikers being raped or even murdered.
• Men are very aggressive in soliciting unaccompanied women but, though offensive, are essentially harmless.

Police assistance:
☎ **100** from any phone

TELEPHONES

Public payphones accept cash and phonecards, and credit cards too in many central city locations. Avoid using hotel phones, which can be expensive. Local codes are: 02 Jerusalem; 03 Tel Aviv; 04 Haifa; 05 mobile phones; 06 North; 07 South; 08 South Central; 09 North Central.
To make direct international calls (possible from public payphones only in tourist areas) you can choose between three different carriers: Golden Lines (012), Barak (013) and Bezeq (014). Rates vary signficantly for each country with each company, so check before dialling. For details of rates, phone free to: Golden Lines ☎ 1 800 1212; Barak ☎ 1 800 1313; Bezeq ☎ 188.

International Dialling Codes			
From Israel 012 or 013 or 014 then:			
UK:	44	Germany:	49
USA & Canada:	1	Netherlands:	31
Spain:	34		

POST

Post offices are identified by a red logo with a white stag. Opening times are 8–12:30 and 3:30–6 (Wed 8–1:30 only); central offices are open through the day. All offices close Friday afternoon and Saturday. Most post boxes are red, though in some cities they are yellow for in-town and red for out-of-town mail.

ELECTRICITY

The power supply is 220 volts. Type of socket: Round three-hole (in triangular formation) sockets (sometimes two) taking plugs of three (or two) round or flat pins. British visitors should bring an adaptor; US visitors a voltage transformer. Hotels usually have universal outlets for shavers.

TIPS/GRATUITIES

Yes ✓   No ✗

Restaurants (if service not inc.)	✓	10%
Bar service	✗	
Taxis	✗	
Tour guides (depending on size of group and time)	✓	
Hairdressers	✗	
Chambermaids	✗	
Porters (hotel)	✓	2/3 shekels a bag
Cloakroom attendants	✗	
Toilet attendants	✗	

What and when to photograph: The landscapes, holy sites and city scenes. Winter, early spring and late autumn offer the best light.
What and when not to photograph: Israelis generally love to be photographed, but ultra-orthodox Jews and devout Muslims see photographs as a prohibited 'graven image'. Do not photograph holy sites or orthodox Jews on the sabbath or festivals. Avoid military installations.
Where to buy film There are plenty of stores selling all the well-known brand names but film is relatively expensive.

HEALTH

 Insurance
A comprehensive travel insurance policy is essential, as hospitalisation is very expensive. Israel's medical system is comparable to Western European Health Services.

 Dental Services
Dentists are plentiful and the standards of Israeli-trained dentists (and their prices) are high. If possible, check where the dentist concerned qualified.

 Sun Advice
The major threat to health in Israel is the sun. Between April and October avoid going outside between 11AM and 3PM. If you must, drink plenty of water, use a high-factor sun lotion, wear a hat, and keep arms and legs covered.

Drugs
Medication is widely available from pharmacies, and most pharmacists speak fluent English. It is the practice in smaller pharmacies to sell drugs over the counter without a prescription, although this is illegal. Everyday medication is relatively cheap but rarer, imported drugs can be very costly.

 Safe Water
It is safe to drink tap water in Israel, although locally bottled spring water is widely available – Mei Eden and Neviot are the largest companies. Beware, some other brands are simply tap water with added minerals.

CONCESSIONS

Students/Youths Holders of valid international Student Identity Cards will receive a 10 per cent discount on buses, 25 per cent on trains and reductions at some museums. The Israel Student Tourist Association (ISSTA), which has a desk at the airport, arranges cheap flights to and from Israel, and a variety of cheaper tours within Israel.

Senior Citizens Senior citizens (women over 60 and men over 65) receive a 50 per cent reduction on buses. The discount is automatically given but proof of identity may sometimes be requested. Museums, cinemas and theatres also offer 50 per cent reductions.

CLOTHING SIZES

Israel	UK	Europe	USA	
46	36	46	36	
48	38	48	38	
50	40	50	40	
52	42	52	42	Suits
54	44	54	44	
56	46	56	46	
41	7	41	8	
42	7.5	42	8.5	
43	8.5	43	9.5	
44	9.5	44	10.5	Shoes
45	10.5	45	11.5	
46	11	46	12	
37	14.5	37	14.5	
38	15	38	15	
39/40	15.5	39/40	15.5	
41	16	41	16	Shirts
42	16.5	42	16.5	
43	17	43	17	
34	8	34	6	
36	10	36	8	
38	12	38	10	
40	14	40	12	Dresses
42	16	42	14	
44	18	44	16	
37.5	4.5	37.5	6	
38	5	38	6.5	
38.5	5.5	38.5	7	
39	6	39	7.5	Shoes
40	6.5	40	8	
41	7	41	8.5	

WHEN DEPARTING

- You should contact the airline at least 72 hours before departure to 'reconfirm' your return flight. Some airlines can delete your name from the passenger list if this procedure is not followed.
- Arrive at the airport at least 2½ hours before departure to allow time for rigorous security checks, or take advantage of the Israel Airport Authority's 'day before' check-in service for baggage.

LANGUAGE

The common language of Israel is Hebrew, although Arabic is also an official language. Ultra-orthodox Jews speak Yiddish (Judeo-German), while more than a million Israelis were born in Russian-speaking countries. Israelis are very adept at languages and almost everybody speaks adequate English. Hebrew is a Semitic language (like Arabic) read from right to left. The following Hebrew words and phrases may be useful but it is usually easier to communicate in English as Israelis may find the awkward pronunciation of your Hebrew more difficult to understand than English. Place-name spelling is not standardised, so the visitor is likely to see several versions in use at once, eg. Safed, Zefat, Tzfat.

hotel	bet malon	shower	miklachat
guest house	bet ha'aracha	bath	ambatia
room	heder	dining room	heder ochel
lift	ma'alit	one night	lailah ahat
door	delet	two nights	shtai lailot
bed	mita	a week	shavua
stairs	madregot	two weeks	shavuaim
toilets	shirutim	a room with a view	heder im nof

one	ahat	twenty	esrim
two	shtayim	thirty	saloshim
three	shalosh	forty	arbaim
four	arba	fifty	hamishim
five	hamesh	hundred	mea
six	shesh	thousand	eleph
seven	sheva	how much?	kama?
eight	shmona	money	ceseph
nine	tesha	change	odeph
ten	eser	bank	bank

restaurant	misada	wine	yayin
café	bet cafe	beer	bira
please	bevakasha	soup	marak
thank you	toda	salad	salat
can I order?	efshar lehazmin	cake	ooga
food	ochel	bread	lehem
drink	shtia	butter	chema
tea	te	cheese	gevina
coffee	cafe	fruit	perot
water	mayim	bill	heshbon

bus	autobus	shared taxi	sherut
bus stop	tahanat autobus	car	recev
ticket	cartis	train	rakevet
taxi	monit	station	tahanat rakevet

hello/goodbye	shalom	what is the time?	ma hasha'a
yes	ken	good morning	boker tov
no	lo	good afternoon	tzohoraim tovim
how are you?	ma Shlomcha?	good evening	erev tov
telephone	telefon	goodnight	lailah tov
when	matay	today	hayom
where	efo	tomorrow	mahar
excuse me	sliha	yesterday	etmol

INDEX

Acknowledgements

The Automobile Association wishes to thank the following photographers, libraries and museum for their assistance in the preparation of this book:

MARY EVANS PICTURE LIBRARY 10b, 11; **ROBERT HARDING PICTURE LIBRARY** 36; **HULTON GETTY** 14b; **ISRAEL MUSEUM, JERUSALEM** 20b; **MRI BANKERS' GUIDE TO FOREIGN CURRENCY** 119; **PAUL MURPHY** 68, 71; **REX FEATURES LTD** 14c; **SPECTRUM COLOUR LIBRARY** f/cover (Dome of the Rock)

The remaining photographs are held in the Association's own library (**AA PHOTO LIBRARY**) and were taken by Pat Aithie, apart from contributions from: Charles Aithie 58, 59; Julian Loader f/cover (Golan Heights), 13, 15a, 16a, 17a, 17b, 18a, 19a, 20a, 21a, 21b, 22a, 23a, 24a, 25a, 26a, 26b, 39b, 42b, 43b, 49b, 83b, 87a, 87b, 90; Tony Souter f/cover (Bedouin artefact), 1, 5a, 6a, 7a, 8a, 9a, 10a, 12a, 14a, 23b, 27b, 46, 72c, 73a, 117b.

Copy editor: Sheila Hawkins   Page layout: Stuart Perry   Revision Management: Pam Stagg